AS A MAN THINKETH

A Journey Through Philosophy, Psychology, and
Theological Wisdom

Dr. Maxwell Shimba

Shimba Publishing LLC

TABLE OF CONTENTS

INTRODUCTION

The concept of "As a Man Thinketh" explores the profound impact of thoughts on one's life. Drawing from philosophy, psychology, and biblical wisdom, this book delves into how our mental landscape shapes our reality and destiny. The notion that our thoughts dictate our circumstances is not new; it has been a cornerstone of philosophical inquiry and spiritual teachings for centuries. However, in our fast-paced modern world, we often overlook the significance of our inner dialogue and its power to mold our experiences.

In this book, we will journey through the realms of philosophy, psychology, and scripture to understand how our thoughts influence every aspect of our being. By examining the wisdom of ancient philosophers, modern psychological theories, and timeless biblical truths, we aim to uncover the mechanisms through which our mental processes create our external world.

Philosophical Insights

Philosophy offers a wealth of knowledge on the nature of thoughts and their power. From the teachings of Socrates, who emphasized the importance of self-examination, to the meditations of Marcus Aurelius, who practiced Stoic resilience, philosophers have long recognized the central role of thought in shaping human existence. This book will explore these philosophical insights, demonstrating how ancient wisdom can be applied to contemporary life.

Psychological Perspectives

Modern psychology provides us with tools and theories that help us understand the intricate workings of the mind. Cognitive-behavioral therapy, for example, shows how changing our thought patterns can lead to significant improvements in mental health and behavior. Positive psychology highlights the benefits of optimism and gratitude, while neuroscience reveals how our thoughts can physically alter our brain structure. By integrating these psychological perspectives, we will gain a deeper understanding of how to harness the power of our thoughts for personal growth and well-being.

Biblical Wisdom

The Bible is rich with teachings that underscore the importance of our inner life. Verses like "For as he thinks in his heart, so is he" (Proverbs 23:7) and "Do not conform to the pattern of this world, but be transformed by the renewing of your mind" (Romans 12:2) emphasize the transformative power of thoughts. Throughout this book, we will draw upon biblical wisdom to illustrate how aligning our thoughts with divine principles can lead to a more fulfilling and purposeful life.

The Journey Ahead

As we embark on this journey, it is essential to approach it with an open mind and a willing heart. The path to mastering our thoughts is not always easy, but it is profoundly rewarding. By understanding the power of our mental landscape, we can take control of our destiny and create a life that reflects our deepest values and aspirations.

Each chapter of this book will delve into a specific aspect of thought and its impact on our lives. We will explore topics such as the influence of beliefs, the creative power of thought, the connection between thoughts and health, and the pursuit of peace and serenity. Along the way, we will encounter stories of individuals who have transformed their lives through the power of positive thinking and learn practical strategies for cultivating a healthy and productive mindset.

In "As a Man Thinketh," we invite you to discover the incredible potential that lies within your mind. By embracing the wisdom of philosophy, psychology, and scripture, you can unlock the secrets to a fulfilling and successful life. Let this book be your guide as you navigate the transformative journey of mastering your thoughts and, in turn, mastering your life.

DR. MAXWELL SHIMBA

THE POWER OF THOUGHT

The concept that our thoughts have a profound influence on our lives is a cornerstone of many philosophical traditions. Ancient philosophers like Socrates and Plato delved deeply into the nature of thoughts, understanding that they are not mere fleeting moments but powerful forces that shape our reality. This chapter will explore their teachings, revealing the enduring wisdom of their insights and how they remain relevant in our modern lives.

Socratic Wisdom

Socrates, often considered the father of Western philosophy, emphasized the importance of self-examination and the pursuit of wisdom. His famous dictum, "The unexamined life is not worth living," underscores the critical role of introspection in personal development. For Socrates, thoughts were not just internal dialogues but the essence of one's character and morality. He believed that by scrutinizing our thoughts and beliefs, we could achieve a deeper understanding of ourselves and the world around us.

Socratic questioning, a method of probing ideas and assumptions through rigorous dialogue, encourages us to reflect on our thoughts critically. This method helps us uncover underlying beliefs that shape our perceptions and actions. By questioning our thoughts and seeking clarity, we can transform our mental landscape and align our actions with our highest values.

Platonic Ideals

Plato, a student of Socrates, expanded on his teacher's ideas and developed a comprehensive philosophy that included the theory of Forms or Ideas. According to Plato, the material world we perceive with our senses is just a shadow of a higher, more perfect reality composed of immutable and eternal Forms. Our thoughts, Plato argued, have the power to access this higher realm and grasp the truth.

In his famous work, "The Republic," Plato presents the allegory of the cave, a powerful metaphor for the transformative power of thought. In the allegory, prisoners are chained in a cave, only able to see shadows cast on the wall by objects behind them. These shadows represent their perception of reality. However, one prisoner escapes and discovers the outside world, realizing that the shadows are mere reflections of the true Forms.

Plato's allegory highlights the potential of our thoughts to transcend the limitations of our immediate perceptions and connect with a higher reality. By cultivating our capacity for abstract thinking and philosophical contemplation, we can rise above the shadows of everyday life and achieve a deeper understanding of truth and existence.

The Power of Thought in Daily Life

The teachings of Socrates and Plato emphasize that our thoughts are not passive occurrences but active agents that shape our character and reality. In modern terms, we might think of this in relation to the concept of the "self-fulfilling prophecy." This psychological phenomenon occurs when our expectations about a situation influence our behavior in a way that causes those expectations to come true. For example, if we constantly think we will fail, our lack of confidence and effort may lead to actual failure, thereby reinforcing our negative beliefs.

Understanding the power of thought empowers us to take control of our mental landscape. By recognizing the influence of our thoughts on our emotions and behaviors, we can begin to cultivate a more positive and constructive mindset. This process involves not only self-reflection but also the intentional practice of replacing negative or limiting thoughts with positive and empowering ones.

Practical Application

To harness the power of thought, consider adopting the following practices inspired by Socratic and Platonic principles:

1. Self-examination: Regularly set aside time for introspection. Ask yourself questions that challenge your assumptions and beliefs. What are your core values? Are your thoughts and actions aligned with them?

2. Mindfulness: Cultivate mindfulness to become more aware of your thoughts and their impact on your emotions and behaviors. Mindfulness practices, such as meditation, can help you observe your thoughts without judgment and gain greater control over them.

3. Positive Affirmations: Replace negative thoughts with positive affirmations. Affirmations are positive statements that you repeat to yourself to reinforce a desired belief or outcome. For example, instead of thinking, "I can't do this," try affirming, "I am capable and confident."

4. Philosophical Inquiry: Engage with philosophical texts and ideas to expand your understanding of thought and reality. Reflect on how the insights of philosophers like Socrates and Plato can be applied to your life.

5. Goal Setting: Set clear, achievable goals that align with your values and aspirations. Visualize yourself achieving these goals and consider the steps you need to take to make them a reality.

Biblical Perspective

The power of thought is also emphasized in the Bible, providing a spiritual dimension to the insights of Socrates and Plato. Proverbs 23:7 states, "For as he thinks in his heart, so is he." This verse highlights the profound influence of our thoughts on our identity and actions. Similarly, Romans 12:2 encourages us to be "transformed by the renewal of your mind," underscoring the transformative potential of aligning our thoughts with divine principles.

By integrating these philosophical and biblical teachings, we can develop a holistic understanding of the power of thought. Our thoughts are not only reflections of our internal world but also catalysts for change in our external reality. Through intentional self-examination, mindfulness, and positive thinking, we can harness this power to create a life that reflects our highest ideals and values.

In the journey of mastering our thoughts, we are not alone. We stand on the shoulders of great thinkers like Socrates and Plato, guided by their wisdom and inspired by their pursuit of truth. As we embark on this journey, let us remember that our thoughts are the seeds of our destiny. By nurturing them with care and intention, we can cultivate a life of purpose, fulfillment, and profound transformation.

The Power of Thought

The concept that our thoughts have a profound influence on our lives is a cornerstone of many philosophical traditions. Ancient philosophers like Socrates and Plato delved deeply into the nature of thoughts, understanding that they are not mere fleeting moments but powerful forces that shape our reality. This chapter will explore their teachings, revealing the enduring wisdom of their insights and how they remain relevant in our modern lives. Additionally, modern psychology provides us with tools and theories that help us understand the intricate workings of the mind, such as cognitive-behavioral theory.

Socrates, often considered the father of Western philosophy, emphasized the importance of self-examination and the pursuit of wisdom. His famous dictum, "The unexamined life is not worth living," underscores the critical role of introspection in personal development. For Socrates, thoughts were not just internal dialogues but the essence of one's character and morality. He believed that by scrutinizing our thoughts and beliefs, we could achieve a deeper understanding of ourselves and the world around us.

Socratic questioning, a method of probing ideas and assumptions through rigorous dialogue, encourages us to reflect on our thoughts critically. This method helps us uncover underlying beliefs that shape our perceptions and actions. By questioning our thoughts and seeking clarity, we can transform our mental landscape and align our actions with our highest values.

Plato, a student of Socrates, expanded on his teacher's ideas and developed a comprehensive philosophy that included the theory of Forms or Ideas. According to Plato, the material world we perceive with our senses is just a shadow of a higher, more perfect reality composed of immutable and eternal Forms. Our thoughts, Plato argued, have the power to access this higher realm and grasp the truth.

In his famous work, "The Republic," Plato presents the allegory of the cave, a powerful metaphor for the transformative power of thought. In the allegory, prisoners are chained in a cave, only able to see shadows cast on the wall by objects behind them. These shadows represent their perception of reality. However, one prisoner escapes and discovers the outside world, realizing that the shadows are mere reflections of the true Forms.

Plato's allegory highlights the potential of our thoughts to transcend the limitations of our immediate perceptions and connect with a higher reality. By cultivating our capacity for abstract thinking and philosophical contemplation, we can rise above the shadows of everyday life and achieve a deeper understanding of truth and existence.

Cognitive-Behavioral Theory: Bridging Philosophy and Psychology

While the insights of Socrates and Plato lay the philosophical groundwork for understanding the power of thought, modern psychology provides practical frameworks for applying these concepts in our daily lives. Cognitive-behavioral theory (CBT) is one such framework that emphasizes the significant impact of our thoughts on our emotions and behaviors.

The Cognitive Triad

At the heart of CBT is the cognitive triad, a model that explains how our thoughts, emotions, and behaviors are interconnected. According to this theory, our thoughts influence our feelings, which in turn affect our actions. For instance, if we have negative thoughts about ourselves or our circumstances, we are likely to experience negative emotions such as anxiety or depression, leading to behaviors that reinforce these negative thoughts.

Automatic Thoughts

CBT posits that many of our thoughts are automatic and often go unnoticed. These automatic thoughts can be positive or negative and are typically influenced by our underlying beliefs and experiences. Negative automatic thoughts, such as "I'm not good enough" or "Nothing ever goes right for me," can create a cycle of negative emotions and behaviors. By identifying and challenging these automatic thoughts, we can break the cycle and develop more positive and constructive patterns of thinking.

Cognitive Distortions

Cognitive distortions are irrational or biased ways of thinking that contribute to negative emotions and behaviors. Common cognitive distortions include:

1. All-or-Nothing Thinking: Viewing situations in black-and-white terms, without recognizing the middle ground.

2. Overgeneralization: Making broad conclusions based on a single event or limited evidence.

3. Catastrophizing: Expecting the worst possible outcome in any situation.

4. Personalization: Blaming oneself for events outside of one's control.

By becoming aware of these cognitive distortions, we can challenge and reframe them, leading to healthier and more balanced thinking patterns.

Practical Application: CBT Techniques

CBT offers several practical techniques for transforming our thoughts and, consequently, our emotions and behaviors. Here are a few key strategies:

1. Cognitive Restructuring: This technique involves identifying and challenging negative automatic thoughts and cognitive distortions. By examining the evidence for and against these thoughts, we can develop more balanced and realistic perspectives.

2. Thought Records: Keeping a thought record can help us track our automatic thoughts and identify patterns. By recording our thoughts, emotions, and behaviors in different situations, we can gain insights into how our thinking influences our feelings and actions.

3. Behavioral Experiments: These involve testing the validity of our thoughts through real-world experiments. For example, if we have a fear of public speaking, we might gradually expose ourselves to speaking in front of small groups to challenge the belief that we will always perform poorly.

4. Mindfulness: Practicing mindfulness can help us become more aware of our thoughts and emotions in the present moment. By observing our thoughts without judgment, we can create space to respond more thoughtfully and less reactively.

Biblical Perspective

The power of thought is also emphasized in the Bible, providing a spiritual dimension to the insights of cognitive-behavioral theory. Proverbs 23:7 states, "For as he thinks in his heart, so is he." This verse highlights the profound influence of our thoughts on our identity and actions. Similarly, Romans 12:2 encourages us to be "transformed by the renewal of your mind," underscoring the transformative potential of aligning our thoughts with divine principles.

By integrating these philosophical, psychological, and biblical teachings, we can develop a holistic understanding of the power of thought. Our thoughts are not only reflections of our internal world but also catalysts for change in our external reality. Through intentional self-examination, mindfulness, and positive thinking, we can harness this power to create a life that reflects our highest ideals and values.

The Journey Ahead

Understanding the power of thought is the first step toward transforming our lives. As we delve deeper into this book, we will explore various aspects of thought and their impact on our existence. By applying the wisdom of ancient philosophers, the practical insights of modern psychology, and the timeless truths of the Bible, we can embark on a journey of personal growth and transformation.

In the journey of mastering our thoughts, we are not alone. We stand on the shoulders of great thinkers like Socrates and Plato, guided by their wisdom and inspired by their pursuit of truth. As we embark on this journey, let us remember that our thoughts are the seeds of our destiny. By nurturing them with care and intention, we can cultivate a life of purpose, fulfillment, and profound transformation.

CHAPTER 02

FOR AS HE THINKS IN HIS HEART, SO IS HE (PROVERBS 23:7)

The Significance of Proverbs 23:7

The verse Proverbs 23:7, "For as he thinks in his heart, so is he," encapsulates a profound truth about the relationship between our thoughts and our identity. This biblical wisdom highlights that our innermost thoughts and beliefs shape who we are and ultimately determine the course of our lives. In this chapter, we will explore the significance of this verse and how it aligns with insights from philosophy and psychology to provide a comprehensive understanding of the power of thought.

Biblical Context and Interpretation

To fully appreciate the depth of Proverbs 23:7, it is essential to consider its context within the Bible. The Book of Proverbs, attributed to King Solomon, is a collection of wise sayings and teachings that offer guidance on living a righteous and meaningful life. This particular verse speaks to the power of inner thought life, suggesting that what we think in our hearts—our true, inner convictions—defines us.

The "heart" in biblical terms often represents the core of our being, encompassing our mind, emotions, and will. Therefore, this verse implies that our internal thoughts and attitudes profoundly influence our external reality. It urges us to cultivate positive and godly thoughts, as they directly shape our character and actions.

Philosophical Parallels

The wisdom of Proverbs 23:7 finds echoes in the teachings of ancient philosophers who also recognized the transformative power of thought. Socrates, for instance, emphasized the importance of self-examination and introspection, believing that understanding our inner world is crucial for leading a virtuous life. His practice of questioning assumptions and beliefs aimed to uncover deeper truths and promote self-awareness.

Plato, Socrates' student, further developed this idea through his theory of Forms, suggesting that our thoughts can connect us to a higher reality. The allegory of the cave illustrates how our perceptions and thoughts shape our understanding of the world. By transcending the shadows of immediate sensory experience and contemplating the eternal Forms, we can attain true knowledge and wisdom.

These philosophical insights align with the message of Proverbs 23:7, reinforcing the idea that our thoughts are not merely passive reflections but active forces that shape our reality and identity.

Psychological Perspectives

Modern psychology, particularly cognitive-behavioral theory (CBT), offers valuable tools for understanding and harnessing the power of thought. CBT posits that our thoughts, emotions, and behaviors are interconnected, and by changing our thought patterns, we can influence our emotional well-being and actions.

Automatic Thoughts and Cognitive Distortions

CBT identifies automatic thoughts as spontaneous, often subconscious thoughts that arise in response to various situations. These thoughts can be positive or negative and are influenced by our underlying beliefs and experiences. Negative automatic thoughts, such as "I'm worthless" or "I'll never succeed," can lead to negative emotions and self-defeating behaviors.

Cognitive distortions are irrational or biased ways of thinking that contribute to negative emotions and behaviors. Common cognitive distortions include:

1. All-or-Nothing Thinking: Viewing situations in black-and-white terms, without recognizing the middle ground.

2. Overgeneralization: Making broad conclusions based on a single event or limited evidence.

3. Catastrophizing: Expecting the worst possible outcome in any situation.

4. Personalization: Blaming oneself for events outside of one's control.

By identifying and challenging these cognitive distortions, we can develop more balanced and realistic thought patterns, leading to improved emotional and behavioral outcomes.

Cognitive Restructuring

Cognitive restructuring is a key technique in CBT that involves identifying negative automatic thoughts and cognitive distortions and replacing them with more positive and realistic thoughts. This process helps to break the cycle of negative thinking and promotes emotional resilience.

Practical Application: Transforming Our Thoughts

To align our thoughts with the wisdom of Proverbs 23:7 and harness their power to shape our identity and reality, consider adopting the following practices:

1. Self-Examination: Regularly set aside time for introspection and self-examination. Reflect on your thoughts and beliefs, and consider how they influence your emotions and behaviors. Ask yourself whether your thoughts align with your values and aspirations.

2. Mindfulness: Cultivate mindfulness to become more aware of your thoughts and their impact on your well-being. Mindfulness practices, such as meditation and deep breathing exercises, can help you observe your thoughts without judgment and create space for intentional responses.

3. Positive Affirmations: Replace negative thoughts with positive affirmations. Affirmations are positive statements that you repeat to yourself to reinforce a desired belief or outcome. For example, instead of thinking, "I can't do this," try affirming, "I am capable and confident."

4. Challenging Cognitive Distortions: Identify and challenge cognitive distortions that contribute to negative thinking patterns. Ask yourself whether your thoughts are based on evidence or whether they reflect irrational or biased ways of thinking. Replace distorted thoughts with more balanced and realistic perspectives.

5. Gratitude Practice: Cultivate a practice of gratitude to shift your focus from negative thoughts to positive ones. Regularly reflecting on the things you are grateful for can help

to reframe your thinking and promote a more positive and optimistic outlook.

Integrating Biblical Wisdom

Integrating the wisdom of Proverbs 23:7 into our daily lives involves more than just intellectual understanding; it requires practical application and spiritual alignment. Here are a few ways to incorporate this biblical truth into your thought life:

1. Scripture Meditation: Meditate on scriptures that emphasize the power of thought and the renewal of the mind. Verses like Romans 12:2 ("Do not conform to the pattern of this world, but be transformed by the renewing of your mind") can serve as reminders to align your thoughts with God's truth.

2. Prayer: Seek God's guidance in transforming your thought life through prayer. Ask for wisdom, discernment, and the ability to recognize and replace negative thoughts with godly ones.

3. Community Support: Engage with a community of like-minded individuals who can provide encouragement and accountability as you work to align your thoughts with biblical principles. Sharing your journey with others can provide valuable insights and support.

The Transformative Journey

The journey of transforming our thoughts is a lifelong process that requires dedication, intentionality, and spiritual alignment. By integrating the insights of Proverbs 23:7 with the teachings of philosophy and psychology, we can develop a holistic approach to mastering our thoughts and shaping our identity.

As we continue to explore the power of thought in this book, let us remember that our thoughts are not merely passive reflections of our inner world but active forces that shape our external reality. By nurturing our thoughts with care and intention, we can cultivate a life of purpose, fulfillment, and profound transformation.

In the chapters ahead, we will delve deeper into various aspects of thought and their impact on our lives, drawing from the wisdom of ancient philosophers, modern psychology, and biblical truths. Together, we will embark on a transformative journey of self-discovery and personal growth, guided by the timeless wisdom of Proverbs 23:7: "For as he thinks in his heart, so is he."

The Inner World

The concept of the inner world, or the inner self, is a cornerstone of many philosophical traditions, both Eastern and Western. It is the seat of our thoughts, emotions, and identity, and it shapes our interactions with the external world.

Understanding and cultivating our inner world is essential for personal growth, self-awareness, and fulfillment. In this chapter, we will examine the idea of the inner self from various philosophical perspectives, drawing from both Eastern and Western traditions to uncover a holistic understanding of this profound concept.

Western Philosophical Traditions

Socrates and the Unexamined Life

Socrates, one of the most influential figures in Western philosophy, famously stated, "The unexamined life is not worth living." For Socrates, the inner world was of paramount importance. He believed that true knowledge and wisdom could only be attained through self-examination and introspection. By questioning our beliefs, values, and motivations, we can gain a deeper understanding of our inner selves and live more authentically.

Socratic questioning, a method of probing one's thoughts and assumptions through rigorous dialogue, encourages us to engage in continuous self-reflection. This process helps us uncover the underlying beliefs that shape our perceptions and actions, allowing us to align our lives with our highest values.

Descartes and the Cogito

René Descartes, a foundational figure in modern Western philosophy, also emphasized the importance of the inner self. His famous assertion, "Cogito, ergo sum" ("I think, therefore I am"), underscores the fundamental role of thought in defining our existence. For Descartes, the act of thinking is the essence of the self, and the inner world of thoughts and consciousness is the foundation of our identity.

Descartes' philosophy encourages us to recognize the centrality of our inner world in shaping our reality. By understanding the nature of our thoughts and the processes of our minds, we can gain insights into the true nature of our existence and our place in the world.

Existentialism and Authenticity

Existentialist philosophers such as Jean-Paul Sartre and Martin Heidegger further explored the concept of the inner self, focusing on themes of authenticity, freedom, and self-determination. Sartre's famous dictum, "Existence precedes essence," suggests that individuals are not born with a predefined nature or purpose. Instead, we create our essence through our choices and actions, guided by our inner self.

Existentialism emphasizes the importance of living authentically, in alignment with our true selves. This requires deep self-reflection and an honest examination of our beliefs, values, and desires. By understanding and embracing our inner world, we can live more meaningfully and exercise our freedom to shape our destiny.

Eastern Philosophical Traditions

Buddhism and the Nature of Mind

In Eastern philosophy, the concept of the inner self is also of great significance. Buddhism, for instance, teaches that understanding the nature of the mind is essential for achieving enlightenment. The Buddha emphasized the importance of mindfulness and meditation as tools for exploring the inner world and attaining self-awareness.

Buddhist philosophy posits that the mind is the source of both suffering and liberation. Our thoughts and perceptions shape our experiences, and by cultivating awareness and wisdom, we can transform our inner world and achieve a state of inner peace and clarity. The practice of mindfulness involves observing our thoughts and emotions without attachment or judgment, allowing us to see the true nature of our mind and transcend its limitations.

Hinduism and the Atman

In Hindu philosophy, the concept of the inner self is closely linked to the idea of the Atman, or the true self. The Upanishads, ancient Hindu scriptures, teach that the Atman is the eternal, unchanging essence of an individual, distinct from the transient physical body and mind. Realizing the

Atman is considered the ultimate goal of spiritual practice, leading to liberation (moksha) from the cycle of birth and death (samsara).

The path to realizing the Atman involves deep introspection, self-inquiry, and meditation. By turning inward and exploring the depths of our inner world, we can uncover our true nature and experience a sense of unity with the divine (Brahman). This inner journey is often guided by the teachings of gurus and spiritual texts, providing a framework for self-discovery and spiritual growth.

Taoism and Inner Harmony

Taoism, an ancient Chinese philosophical tradition, also emphasizes the importance of the inner self and inner harmony. The Tao, or the Way, is considered the fundamental principle that underlies the universe and all of existence. Taoist philosophy teaches that by aligning our inner world with the Tao, we can achieve a state of harmony and balance.

Central to Taoist practice is the concept of wu wei, or effortless action. This involves cultivating a state of inner stillness and receptivity, allowing us to act in accordance with the natural flow of the Tao. Through practices such as meditation, qigong, and contemplation, Taoism encourages us to explore our inner world and develop a deep sense of inner peace and harmony.

Integrating Eastern and Western Perspectives

While Eastern and Western philosophical traditions offer distinct approaches to understanding the inner self, they share a common recognition of its importance. Both traditions emphasize the need for self-examination, mindfulness, and inner awareness as essential components of personal growth and fulfillment.

By integrating insights from both Eastern and Western philosophies, we can develop a holistic approach to exploring and cultivating our inner world. This involves:

1. Self-Examination and Reflection: Engage in regular self-examination and reflection to gain insights into your thoughts, beliefs, and motivations. This practice, inspired by Socratic questioning and existentialist introspection, helps you uncover the underlying patterns that shape your inner world.

2. Mindfulness and Meditation: Cultivate mindfulness and meditation practices to develop awareness of your thoughts and emotions. Inspired by Buddhist and Taoist traditions, these practices allow you to observe your inner world without attachment or judgment, fostering inner peace and clarity.

3. Inner Harmony and Balance: Strive to achieve inner harmony and balance by aligning your thoughts and actions

with your true self. This principle, rooted in both Taoism and existentialism, encourages you to live authentically and in accordance with your deepest values.

4. Spiritual Inquiry: Explore spiritual teachings and practices that resonate with you, whether from Hinduism, Buddhism, Taoism, or other traditions. Spiritual inquiry can provide valuable insights into the nature of the inner self and guide you on your journey of self-discovery and growth.

Practical Application: Cultivating Your Inner World

To cultivate your inner world and align your life with your true self, consider adopting the following practices:

1. Journaling: Keep a journal to record your thoughts, reflections, and insights. Journaling can help you clarify your thoughts, identify patterns, and track your progress on your journey of self-discovery.

2. Mindfulness Exercises: Practice mindfulness exercises, such as mindful breathing or body scans, to develop present-moment awareness and observe your inner world without judgment.

3. Meditation: Set aside regular time for meditation to explore the depths of your inner self. Experiment with different meditation techniques, such as focused attention, loving-kindness, or insight meditation, to find what works best for you.

4. Contemplation: Engage in contemplative practices, such as reading and reflecting on philosophical or spiritual texts. Contemplation can deepen your understanding of the inner self and provide inspiration for your personal growth.

5. Inner Dialogue: Practice inner dialogue by engaging in self-questioning and reflection. Ask yourself probing questions about your thoughts, beliefs, and motivations, and consider how they align with your true self and values.

6. Spiritual Practices: Incorporate spiritual practices that resonate with you, such as prayer, chanting, or ritual. These practices can help you connect with your inner self and the divine, fostering a sense of unity and purpose.

The journey of exploring and cultivating the inner world is a deeply personal and transformative process. By drawing from the wisdom of both Eastern and Western philosophical traditions, we can develop a comprehensive understanding of the inner self and its profound impact on our lives.

As we continue to delve into the power of thought and the nature of the inner world, let us remember that true growth and fulfillment come from within. By nurturing our inner selves with care, intention, and mindfulness, we can create a life that reflects our highest values and deepest aspirations. Through this journey of self-discovery, we can achieve a state of inner harmony and realize the true essence of who we are.

The Role of the Subconscious Mind

The human mind is a complex and multifaceted entity, comprising both conscious and subconscious components. While our conscious mind governs our immediate awareness and deliberate actions, the subconscious mind operates beneath the surface, influencing our perceptions, behaviors, and emotional responses in profound ways. In this chapter, we will explore the nature of the subconscious mind, its role in shaping our lives, and how we can harness its power for personal growth and transformation.

The Nature of the Subconscious Mind

The subconscious mind is a repository of thoughts, memories, beliefs, and experiences that are not in our immediate awareness but nevertheless influence our behavior and perception. It operates autonomously, managing processes and responses without our conscious direction. This aspect of the mind is critical for survival, as it automates routine tasks and reactions, allowing the conscious mind to focus on novel and complex challenges.

Freud's Model of the Mind

Sigmund Freud, the father of psychoanalysis, introduced the concept of the subconscious mind as part of his tripartite model of the psyche, which also includes the conscious and unconscious mind. According to Freud, the subconscious mind acts as a gatekeeper, controlling the flow of information between the conscious and unconscious realms. It stores repressed memories and unresolved conflicts, which can manifest in dreams, slips of the tongue, and various behaviors.

Freud's model emphasizes that many of our actions and emotional responses are driven by subconscious motivations. By bringing these hidden influences into conscious awareness through techniques such as free association and dream analysis, we can gain insight into our underlying desires and conflicts, facilitating personal healing and growth.

Cognitive Psychology and the Subconscious

Cognitive psychology has further expanded our understanding of the subconscious mind, highlighting its role in information processing, memory, and learning. Cognitive processes such as pattern recognition, implicit memory, and automaticity are all functions of the subconscious mind.

Implicit Memory and Learning

Implicit memory refers to the unconscious retention of information and skills, which influences our behavior without explicit awareness. This type of memory is involved in tasks such as riding a bicycle, typing on a keyboard, or driving a car, where learned behaviors become automatic through repetition and practice.

Implicit learning occurs when we acquire knowledge or skills without conscious effort or awareness. For example, we might pick up social cues, cultural norms, or language patterns through observation and interaction, integrating this information into our subconscious mind.

Automaticity and Habit Formation

Automaticity is the process by which behaviors become automatic through repetition and practice. The subconscious mind plays a crucial role in habit formation, where repeated actions become ingrained patterns that operate without conscious thought. Habits can be both beneficial, such as regular exercise or healthy eating, and detrimental, such as smoking or procrastination.

By understanding the mechanisms of automaticity and habit formation, we can develop strategies to cultivate positive habits and break negative ones. This involves identifying triggers, creating new routines, and reinforcing desired behaviors through repetition and positive reinforcement.

The Subconscious and Perception

The subconscious mind significantly influences our perceptions and interpretations of the world around us. Our beliefs, past experiences, and emotional states shape how we perceive and respond to external stimuli.

Cognitive Biases

Cognitive biases are systematic patterns of deviation from rational judgment, which occur due to the influence of the subconscious mind. These biases affect our perception, decision-making, and behavior. Some common cognitive biases include:

1. Confirmation Bias: The tendency to seek, interpret, and remember information that confirms our preexisting beliefs and ignore or discount contradictory evidence.

2. Anchoring Bias: The tendency to rely heavily on the first piece of information encountered (the "anchor") when making decisions, even if it is irrelevant.

3. Availability Heuristic: The tendency to overestimate the likelihood of events based on their availability in memory, influenced by recent or emotionally charged experiences.

By becoming aware of these biases, we can work to mitigate their effects and make more rational and objective decisions.

Emotional Influences

Emotions play a significant role in shaping our perceptions and actions, often operating at a subconscious level. For instance, past traumatic experiences can create subconscious emotional responses that influence our behavior and interactions. Similarly, positive emotions such as love, joy, and gratitude can enhance our perception and well-being.

Understanding the interplay between emotions and the subconscious mind allows us to manage our emotional responses more effectively. Techniques such as mindfulness, emotional regulation, and cognitive-behavioral therapy (CBT) can help us cultivate positive emotional states and address negative patterns.

Techniques for Accessing and Transforming the Subconscious

Accessing and transforming the subconscious mind involves bringing its contents into conscious awareness and reshaping our underlying beliefs and patterns. Several psychological techniques can facilitate this process:

Hypnosis

Hypnosis is a state of focused attention and heightened suggestibility, where the conscious mind becomes more receptive to accessing the subconscious. Hypnotherapy uses guided relaxation and suggestion to explore subconscious thoughts and beliefs, facilitating therapeutic change and personal growth.

Meditation and Mindfulness

Meditation and mindfulness practices cultivate present-moment awareness and help us observe our thoughts and emotions without judgment. By quieting the conscious mind, we can gain insight into our subconscious patterns and develop greater self-awareness and inner peace.

Journaling

Journaling is a powerful tool for accessing the subconscious mind. By writing down our thoughts, feelings, and experiences, we can uncover hidden patterns and gain clarity on our inner world. Reflective journaling encourages self-exploration and can reveal insights that lead to personal transformation.

Dream Analysis

Dreams are a window into the subconscious mind, often reflecting unresolved conflicts, desires, and emotions. Analyzing dreams can provide valuable insights into our inner world and help us understand the underlying motivations and issues that influence our behavior.

Cognitive-Behavioral Therapy (CBT)

CBT is an evidence-based therapeutic approach that focuses on identifying and challenging negative thought patterns and beliefs. By bringing subconscious thoughts into conscious awareness and restructuring them, CBT helps individuals develop healthier cognitive and behavioral responses.

Practical Application: Harnessing the Power of the Subconscious

To harness the power of the subconscious mind for personal growth and transformation, consider incorporating the following practices into your daily routine:

1. Mindfulness Meditation: Set aside time each day for mindfulness meditation to develop present-moment awareness and observe your thoughts and emotions without judgment.

2. Reflective Journaling: Keep a journal to explore your thoughts, feelings, and experiences. Reflect on recurring patterns and insights that emerge, and use this information to guide your personal growth.

3. Affirmations and Visualization: Use positive affirmations and visualization techniques to reprogram your subconscious mind. Visualize your goals and aspirations as already achieved, reinforcing positive beliefs and attitudes.

4. Emotional Regulation: Practice techniques for regulating your emotions, such as deep breathing, progressive muscle relaxation, and grounding exercises. Managing your

emotional responses helps create a balanced and positive inner world.

5. Dream Journaling: Keep a dream journal to record and analyze your dreams. Reflect on the symbols and themes that appear, and consider how they relate to your waking life and subconscious mind.

6. Therapeutic Support: Seek support from a therapist or counselor, especially if you are dealing with deep-seated issues or trauma. Therapeutic approaches such as CBT, hypnotherapy, or psychoanalysis can provide valuable insights and facilitate healing.

The subconscious mind is a powerful and influential aspect of our inner world, shaping our perceptions, behaviors, and emotional responses. By understanding and accessing the subconscious, we can uncover hidden patterns, beliefs, and motivations that influence our lives. Through practices such as mindfulness, journaling, and therapeutic support, we can harness the power of the subconscious mind for personal growth and transformation.

As we continue to explore the inner world and the power of thought in this book, let us remember that our subconscious mind is a valuable ally in our journey of self-discovery and fulfillment. By cultivating awareness and intentionally shaping our inner landscape, we can create a life that reflects our true potential and deepest aspirations.

Guarding the Heart

The heart, in biblical terms, is often seen as the center of our being, encompassing our thoughts, emotions, desires, and will. Proverbs 4:23 advises us to "guard your heart, for everything you do flows from it." This wisdom highlights the importance of protecting our inner world, as it profoundly influences our actions and character. In this chapter, we will explore the significance of guarding the heart, drawing from philosophy, psychology, and biblical teachings to understand how we can nurture and protect our innermost selves.

The Heart in Biblical Context

In the Bible, the heart is not merely a physical organ but a symbol of our inner life and spiritual condition. It is the seat of our thoughts, emotions, and moral choices. Guarding the heart involves being vigilant about what we allow to influence our inner world, as it shapes our character and actions.

Old Testament Wisdom

The book of Proverbs is rich with teachings about the heart. Proverbs 4:23 emphasizes the importance of guarding the heart because it is the wellspring of life. Similarly, Proverbs 23:7 states, "For as he thinks in his heart, so is he," underscoring the idea that our inner thoughts and beliefs determine our identity and behavior.

New Testament Teachings

In the New Testament, Jesus emphasizes the importance of the heart in our spiritual life. In Matthew 5:8, He says, "Blessed are the pure in heart, for they will see God." This beatitude highlights the value of a pure heart in our relationship with God and our ability to perceive spiritual truths. Furthermore, Jesus teaches that our words and actions reflect the condition of our heart: "For the mouth speaks what the heart is full of" (Luke 6:45).

Philosophical Perspectives on Guarding the Heart

Philosophers throughout history have recognized the importance of cultivating and protecting the inner self. Their teachings provide valuable insights into how we can guard our hearts and maintain inner integrity.

Stoicism and Emotional Resilience

Stoic philosophers like Epictetus and Marcus Aurelius emphasized the importance of inner resilience and emotional regulation. They taught us that we should focus on what is within our control—our thoughts, attitudes, and responses—while accepting what is outside our control. By cultivating inner virtues such as wisdom, courage, and temperance, we can guard our hearts against external disturbances and maintain a state of inner peace.

Plato's Tripartite Soul

Plato's model of the tripartite soul divides the human psyche into three parts: the rational, the spirited, and the appetitive. The rational part seeks truth and wisdom, the spirited part seeks honor and courage, and the appetitive part seeks physical pleasures and desires. Plato believed that a well-ordered soul, governed by reason, leads to a virtuous and harmonious life. Guarding the heart involves ensuring that our rational mind guides our desires and emotions, fostering a balanced and virtuous inner life.

Existentialism and Authenticity

Existentialist philosophers such as Jean-Paul Sartre and Søren Kierkegaard emphasized the importance of living authentically, in alignment with one's true self. They argued that individuals must take responsibility for their choices and live according to their deepest values and beliefs. Guarding the heart in this context means being true to oneself and resisting external pressures to conform, thereby living a life of integrity and authenticity.

Psychological Insights into Guarding the Heart

Psychology offers valuable tools and strategies for understanding and protecting our inner world. By examining the interplay between thoughts, emotions, and behaviors, we can develop effective ways to guard our hearts and nurture our well-being.

Cognitive-Behavioral Therapy (CBT)

CBT is a widely used therapeutic approach that focuses on identifying and challenging negative thought patterns and beliefs. It helps individuals develop healthier cognitive and emotional responses, promoting mental and emotional well-being. Guarding the heart through CBT involves:

1. Identifying Cognitive Distortions: Recognizing and challenging irrational or negative thought patterns that undermine our inner peace and self-esteem.

2. Reframing Thoughts: Replacing negative thoughts with positive and realistic ones, fostering a more balanced and constructive inner dialogue.

3. Developing Coping Strategies: Learning techniques to manage stress, anxiety, and negative emotions, thereby protecting our inner world from external pressures.

Mindfulness and Emotional Regulation

Mindfulness practices cultivate present-moment awareness and help us observe our thoughts and emotions without judgment. By developing mindfulness, we can:

1. Enhance Self-Awareness: Become more attuned to our inner experiences and recognize when negative influences or emotions arise.

2. Regulate Emotions: Develop skills to manage and respond to emotions in a healthy and balanced way, preventing them from overwhelming our inner peace.

3. Cultivate Compassion: Foster self-compassion and empathy, nurturing a positive and supportive inner environment.

Positive Psychology

Positive psychology focuses on enhancing well-being and cultivating strengths and virtues. It encourages us to focus on the positive aspects of our lives and develop practices that promote happiness and fulfillment. Guarding the heart through positive psychology involves:

1. Practicing Gratitude: Regularly reflecting on and expressing gratitude for the positive aspects of our lives, which fosters a positive mindset and emotional resilience.

2. Cultivating Optimism: Developing a hopeful and optimistic outlook on life, which can buffer against stress and adversity.

3. Building Strong Relationships: Nurturing supportive and meaningful relationships that provide emotional support and enhance our well-being.

Practical Strategies for Guarding the Heart

To guard our hearts effectively, we can incorporate various practical strategies into our daily lives. These practices help protect our inner world from negative influences and cultivate a positive and resilient mindset.

Set Boundaries

Establishing and maintaining healthy boundaries is essential for protecting our inner world. This involves:

1. Emotional Boundaries: Recognizing and respecting our emotional limits, and avoiding situations or relationships that drain our energy or cause undue stress.

2. Mental Boundaries: Being mindful of the information we consume, such as news, social media, and entertainment, and choosing content that supports our well-being and growth.

3. Physical Boundaries: Taking care of our physical health and well-being, which directly impacts our mental and emotional state.

Practice Self-Reflection

Regular self-reflection helps us stay connected with our inner selves and maintain awareness of our thoughts and emotions. This practice involves:

1. Journaling: Writing down our thoughts, feelings, and experiences to gain insight into our inner world and track our personal growth.

2. Meditation: Setting aside time for meditation to quiet the mind, observe our inner experiences, and cultivate a state of inner peace.

3. Prayer: Engaging in prayer or spiritual practices that connect us with our faith and provide a sense of guidance and support.

Cultivate Positive Influences

Surrounding ourselves with positive influences supports our efforts to guard our hearts and nurture our well-being. This involves:

1. Building Supportive Relationships: Seeking out relationships that provide emotional support, encouragement, and positivity.

2. Engaging in Uplifting Activities: Participating in activities that bring joy, fulfillment, and a sense of purpose, such as hobbies, volunteer work, or creative pursuits.

3. Fostering a Positive Environment: Creating a physical and emotional environment that promotes peace, positivity, and growth.

Guarding our hearts is a vital aspect of personal growth and spiritual well-being. By protecting our inner world from negative influences and nurturing a positive and resilient mindset, we can live a life that reflects our true values and aspirations. Drawing from biblical wisdom, philosophical insights, and psychological strategies, we can develop practical ways to guard our hearts and cultivate a life of integrity, authenticity, and fulfillment.

As we continue to explore the power of thought and the inner world in this book, let us remember that our hearts are the wellspring of our lives. By guarding our hearts with care, intention, and mindfulness, we can create a life that flows with purpose, peace, and joy.

CHAPTER 03

THE INFLUENCE OF BELIEFS

Beliefs are powerful determinants of human experience, guiding our perceptions, actions, and interactions with the world. They form the bedrock of our identity, influencing how we interpret reality and make decisions. This chapter explores the role of belief systems in shaping human experience from both existentialist and phenomenological perspectives, examining how our beliefs can either empower or constrain us.

Existentialist Perspectives on Belief

Existentialism, a philosophical movement that emphasizes individual freedom, choice, and responsibility, provides profound insights into the nature and influence of beliefs. Existentialists argue that beliefs are not merely passive reflections of reality but active constructions that shape our existence.

Søren Kierkegaard: The Leap of Faith

Søren Kierkegaard, often regarded as the father of existentialism, emphasized the importance of personal belief and faith. He argued that true belief requires a "leap of faith," a commitment that goes beyond rational evidence and embraces the uncertainties of life. For Kierkegaard, beliefs are deeply personal and subjective, shaping our identity and purpose. This leap of faith is an existential choice that defines our relationship with the world and with God, highlighting the transformative power of personal conviction.

Jean-Paul Sartre: Radical Freedom and Responsibility

Jean-Paul Sartre, a prominent existentialist, asserted that humans are condemned to be free. He believed that we are constantly faced with choices and that our beliefs play a crucial role in shaping these choices. According to Sartre, our beliefs are not predetermined by external factors; rather, we create them through our actions and decisions. This perspective emphasizes the active role of individuals in constructing their belief systems and underscores the responsibility that comes with this freedom. Sartre's notion of "bad faith"—the denial of our freedom and responsibility by adopting false beliefs—highlights the dangers of self-deception and the importance of authentic belief.

Simone de Beauvoir: The Ethics of Ambiguity

Simone de Beauvoir extended existentialist ideas to the realm of ethics, exploring how beliefs shape our moral framework. In "The Ethics of Ambiguity," she argued that while our beliefs provide a basis for action, they must be continually examined and re-evaluated in the light of new experiences and insights. De Beauvoir emphasized the dynamic and evolving nature of belief systems, suggesting that authentic beliefs are those that remain open to growth and change. Her work highlights the ethical implications of our beliefs and the importance of living in accordance with our deepest values.

Phenomenological Perspectives on Belief

Phenomenology, a philosophical approach that focuses on the structures of experience and consciousness, offers a different lens through which to understand the influence of beliefs. Phenomenologists explore how beliefs shape our perception of reality and how they are experienced in our everyday lives.

Edmund Husserl: The Intentionality of Belief

Edmund Husserl, the founder of phenomenology, introduced the concept of intentionality, which refers to the directedness of consciousness towards objects and experiences. According to Husserl, beliefs are intentional acts that shape our perception of the world. Our beliefs determine how we interpret and engage with our experiences, influencing our understanding of reality. This perspective emphasizes the active role of belief in structuring our experience and highlights the interplay between belief and perception.

Maurice Merleau-Ponty: Embodied Belief

Maurice Merleau-Ponty, a key figure in phenomenology, emphasized the embodied nature of human experience. He argued that our beliefs are not abstract or detached but are lived and experienced through our bodies. For Merleau-Ponty, beliefs are embedded in our bodily practices and interactions with the world, shaping our perception and behavior. This embodied perspective underscores the holistic nature of belief, highlighting how it influences not only our thoughts but also our physical actions and sensory experiences.

Martin Heidegger: Being-in-the-World

Martin Heidegger's phenomenological approach to belief focuses on the concept of "being-in-the-world." Heidegger argued that our beliefs are integral to our existence and are deeply intertwined with our sense of being. He introduced the idea of "thrownness," suggesting that we are born into a world with pre-existing beliefs and cultural norms that shape our initial understanding of reality. However,

Heidegger also emphasized the possibility of authentic belief, where individuals actively engage with and reinterpret these inherited beliefs in a way that reflects their true self. This perspective highlights the existential and contextual nature of belief, emphasizing its role in our ongoing process of self-discovery and meaning-making.

The Interplay Between Belief and Experience

The existentialist and phenomenological perspectives offer valuable insights into how beliefs shape human experience. By examining the interplay between belief and experience, we can better understand the dynamic and reciprocal relationship between our inner convictions and our external reality.

Beliefs as Filters of Perception

Our beliefs act as filters through which we perceive and interpret the world. They influence what we pay attention to, how we interpret events, and how we respond to challenges. For example, a person who believes in their own worth and potential is more likely to seize opportunities and overcome obstacles, whereas someone with self-limiting beliefs may avoid taking risks and remain stuck in a cycle of self-doubt. This filtering effect underscores the importance of cultivating positive and empowering beliefs.

The Self-Fulfilling Prophecy

Beliefs have the power to become self-fulfilling prophecies, where our expectations influence our actions and ultimately bring about the expected outcome. This phenomenon is well-documented in psychology, where positive beliefs about oneself can lead to increased motivation and success, while negative beliefs can result in self-sabotage and failure. By understanding this dynamic, we can recognize the potential of our beliefs to shape our reality and take steps to align our beliefs with our goals and aspirations.

Belief Transformation

Transforming our beliefs is a crucial aspect of personal growth and self-improvement. This process involves:

1. Self-Reflection: Examining our existing beliefs and their origins, and considering how they influence our behavior and perceptions.

2. Challenging Limiting Beliefs: Identifying and questioning beliefs that constrain our potential, and replacing them with more positive and empowering alternatives.

3. Reinforcement: Practicing new beliefs through positive affirmations, visualization, and consistent action, reinforcing them until they become ingrained in our mindset.

Biblical Insights on Belief

The Bible offers profound wisdom on the nature and influence of beliefs. Biblical teachings emphasize the transformative power of faith and the importance of aligning our beliefs with spiritual truths.

Faith as a Source of Strength

In the New Testament, Jesus frequently emphasized the power of faith. For example, in Matthew 17:20, He says, "Truly I tell you, if you have faith as small as a mustard seed, you can say to this mountain, 'Move from here to there,' and it will move. Nothing will be impossible for you." This teaching highlights the extraordinary potential of belief to bring about change and overcome obstacles.

Renewing the Mind

Romans 12:2 encourages believers to "be transformed by the renewing of your mind." This verse underscores the importance of continually examining and renewing our beliefs in light of spiritual wisdom. By aligning our beliefs with God's truth, we can experience profound transformation and growth.

Guarding the Heart

Proverbs 4:23, "Above all else, guard your heart, for everything you do flows from it," emphasizes the need to protect our inner beliefs and values. This biblical wisdom aligns with the philosophical and psychological insights explored in this chapter, highlighting the central role of belief in shaping our character and actions.

Beliefs are powerful forces that shape our experience of reality, influencing our thoughts, emotions, and actions. By exploring the role of belief systems from existentialist and phenomenological perspectives, we gain a deeper understanding of how our beliefs construct our world and define our identity. Drawing on biblical teachings, we see the transformative potential of aligning our beliefs with spiritual truths and cultivating a mindset of faith and empowerment.

As we continue our journey through this book, let us remember that our beliefs are not fixed but can be examined, challenged, and transformed. By nurturing positive and empowering beliefs, we can create a life that reflects our highest aspirations and deepest values, experiencing the fullness of our potential as individuals and spiritual beings.

Beliefs shape our perceptions, decisions, and interactions, acting as a foundational framework for our understanding of the world. This chapter delves into the impact of core beliefs on mental health and behavior, examining how deeply held convictions influence our emotional well-being and actions. Drawing from psychological theories and empirical research, we will explore how core beliefs can either support or undermine our mental health and how we can cultivate healthier belief systems.

The Nature of Core Beliefs

Core beliefs are fundamental, deeply held views about ourselves, others, and the world. They are often formed early in life and become entrenched through repeated experiences and reinforcement. These beliefs are not always conscious but influence our thoughts, emotions, and behaviors in significant ways.

Formation of Core Beliefs

Core beliefs develop through a combination of early life experiences, cultural influences, and personal reflections. They are often shaped by significant relationships, such as those with parents, caregivers, and peers. Positive experiences and affirmations can lead to healthy core beliefs, while negative experiences, trauma, or consistent criticism can result in maladaptive core beliefs.

Examples of Core Beliefs

Core beliefs can be broadly categorized into three areas:

1. Beliefs about the Self: These include perceptions of self-worth, competence, and identity. Examples include "I am capable," "I am unworthy," or "I am lovable."

2. Beliefs about Others: These encompass our expectations and trust in other people. Examples include "People are trustworthy," "People are dangerous," or "People will betray me."

3. Beliefs about the World: These involve our views on the nature of the world and our place in it. Examples include "The world is a safe place," "The world is unpredictable," or "Life is unfair."

Impact of Core Beliefs on Mental Health

Core beliefs profoundly influence mental health by shaping how we interpret and respond to experiences. They act as filters, coloring our perceptions and reactions, and can either contribute to psychological resilience or vulnerability.

Positive Core Beliefs and Mental Health

Healthy core beliefs foster a positive self-image, constructive relationships, and a hopeful outlook on life. They contribute to psychological resilience, helping individuals cope with stress and adversity. For example:

- Self-Worth: Believing in one's worth and capabilities can enhance self-esteem and confidence, leading to proactive behaviors and achievements.

- Trust in Others: Believing in the goodness and reliability of others can foster supportive relationships and social connectedness, which are crucial for mental well-being.

- Optimism: Viewing the world as a place of opportunities and growth can motivate individuals to pursue goals and embrace challenges, enhancing life satisfaction.

Negative Core Beliefs and Mental Health

Maladaptive core beliefs, on the other hand, can contribute to various mental health issues by perpetuating negative thought patterns and emotional distress. Common negative core beliefs and their impact include:

- Low Self-Esteem: Beliefs like "I am unworthy" or "I am a failure" can lead to persistent feelings of inadequacy, depression, and anxiety.

- Distrust of Others: Beliefs such as "People are dangerous" or "I cannot trust anyone" can result in social withdrawal, loneliness, and relationship difficulties.

- Pessimism: Believing that "The world is a harsh place" or "Nothing good ever happens" can foster chronic stress, hopelessness, and a lack of motivation.

Cognitive-Behavioral Theory and Core Beliefs

Cognitive-Behavioral Therapy (CBT) is a widely used psychological approach that addresses the interplay between thoughts, emotions, and behaviors. CBT posits that core beliefs are central to cognitive patterns and can be modified to improve mental health.

Cognitive Triad

CBT identifies a cognitive triad of negative thoughts that commonly occur in depression and anxiety: negative views of the self, the world, and the future. These thoughts are rooted in maladaptive core beliefs, which maintain and exacerbate emotional distress.

Automatic Thoughts and Core Beliefs

Core beliefs give rise to automatic thoughts, which are immediate, involuntary thoughts in response to situations. For example, a person with the core belief "I am unlovable" might automatically think "She doesn't like me" when someone does not respond to a message promptly. Recognizing and challenging these automatic thoughts is a key component of CBT.

Cognitive Restructuring

CBT techniques, such as cognitive restructuring, aim to identify, challenge, and modify negative core beliefs. This process involves:

1. Identifying Core Beliefs: Through self-reflection and therapeutic dialogue, individuals uncover the underlying beliefs that drive their thoughts and behaviors.

2. Challenging Core Beliefs: Individuals examine the evidence for and against their core beliefs, considering alternative perspectives and interpretations.

3. Forming New Beliefs: By developing more balanced and realistic beliefs, individuals can shift their cognitive patterns and improve their mental health.

Empirical Research on Core Beliefs and Mental Health

Empirical studies support the link between core beliefs and mental health, demonstrating how interventions targeting core beliefs can lead to significant improvements in psychological well-being.

Depression and Core Beliefs

Research has shown that negative core beliefs, particularly those related to self-worth and helplessness, are strongly associated with depression. Studies indicate that CBT interventions focusing on these beliefs can reduce depressive symptoms and prevent relapse.

Anxiety Disorders and Core Beliefs

Core beliefs about vulnerability, danger, and control are central to anxiety disorders. For example, individuals with generalized anxiety disorder (GAD) often hold beliefs like "I cannot handle uncertainty" or "I must always be in control." CBT strategies that challenge these beliefs have been effective in reducing anxiety symptoms.

Eating Disorders and Core Beliefs

Eating disorders are frequently linked to core beliefs about body image, self-worth, and control. Cognitive-behavioral interventions that address these underlying beliefs have been shown to improve treatment outcomes and support long-term recovery.

Practical Strategies for Modifying Core Beliefs

Modifying core beliefs requires a commitment to self-awareness, reflection, and practice. Here are some practical strategies to help individuals reshape their core beliefs:

Self-Reflection and Journaling

Keeping a journal can help individuals track their thoughts and identify recurring patterns linked to core beliefs. Reflecting on these patterns can provide insights into how beliefs influence emotions and behaviors.

Challenging Negative Thoughts

Actively questioning negative automatic thoughts and considering alternative interpretations can weaken the hold of maladaptive core beliefs. This involves:

1. Evidence Gathering: Examining the evidence that supports or contradicts the negative thought.

2. Alternative Explanations: Generating more balanced and realistic interpretations of the situation.

3. Behavioral Experiments: Testing new beliefs through actions and observing the outcomes.

Affirmations and Positive Self-Talk

Using positive affirmations and self-talk can reinforce new, healthier core beliefs. Repeating statements like "I am worthy," "I can trust others," and "The world is full of opportunities" can gradually shift cognitive patterns.

Therapeutic Support

Working with a therapist, particularly one trained in CBT, can provide structured guidance and support in identifying and modifying core beliefs. Therapy offers a safe space for exploring deeply held convictions and developing healthier cognitive frameworks.

Biblical Insights on Belief

The Bible offers wisdom on the transformative power of belief and the importance of aligning our thoughts with spiritual truths. Biblical teachings emphasize faith, hope, and love as foundational beliefs that shape our lives.

Faith and Transformation

Hebrews 11:1 defines faith as "confidence in what we hope for and assurance about what we do not see." This verse highlights the power of belief in shaping our reality and guiding our actions. Faith, as a positive and hopeful belief, can lead to profound transformation and resilience.

Renewing the Mind

Romans 12:2 encourages believers to "be transformed by the renewing of your mind." This verse underscores the importance of continually examining and renewing our beliefs in light of spiritual wisdom. Aligning our beliefs with God's truth can lead to inner peace and fulfillment.

Guarding the Heart

Proverbs 4:23, "Above all else, guard your heart, for everything you do flows from it," emphasizes the need to protect our inner beliefs and values. This biblical wisdom aligns with psychological insights, highlighting the central role of belief in shaping our character and actions.

Core beliefs are powerful determinants of mental health and behavior, influencing our thoughts, emotions, and actions. By understanding the nature and impact of these beliefs, we can take steps to cultivate healthier cognitive patterns and enhance our well-being. Through self-reflection, cognitive restructuring, and therapeutic support, we can transform negative core beliefs and develop a more positive and resilient mindset.

As we continue our exploration of the influence of beliefs, let us remember the wisdom of biblical teachings and the insights of psychological theories. By aligning our beliefs with spiritual truths and fostering positive cognitive frameworks, we can create a life that reflects our highest aspirations and deepest values.

Beliefs shape our perceptions, decisions, and interactions, forming the bedrock of our identity and influencing our mental health and behavior. This chapter explores the profound impact of core beliefs on our lives, drawing insights from psychology and biblical wisdom. We will analyze how deeply held convictions affect our emotional well-being and actions, and how we can cultivate healthier belief systems to empower ourselves.

The Nature of Core Beliefs

Core beliefs are fundamental, deeply held views about ourselves, others, and the world. These beliefs are often formed early in life and become entrenched through repeated experiences and reinforcement. While they are not always conscious, they significantly influence our thoughts, emotions, and behaviors.

Formation of Core Beliefs

Core beliefs develop through a combination of early life experiences, cultural influences, and personal reflections. Significant relationships, such as those with parents, caregivers, and peers, shape these beliefs. Positive experiences and affirmations can lead to healthy core beliefs, while negative experiences, trauma, or consistent criticism can result in maladaptive core beliefs.

Examples of Core Beliefs

Core beliefs can be broadly categorized into three areas:

1. Beliefs about the Self: These include perceptions of self-worth, competence, and identity. Examples include "I am capable," "I am unworthy," or "I am lovable."

2. Beliefs about Others: These encompass our expectations and trust in other people. Examples include "People are trustworthy," "People are dangerous," or "People will betray me."

3. Beliefs about the World: These involve our views on the nature of the world and our place in it. Examples include "The world is a safe place," "The world is unpredictable," or "Life is unfair."

Impact of Core Beliefs on Mental Health

Core beliefs profoundly influence mental health by shaping how we interpret and respond to experiences. They act as filters, coloring our perceptions and reactions, and can either contribute to psychological resilience or vulnerability.

Positive Core Beliefs and Mental Health

Healthy core beliefs foster a positive self-image, constructive relationships, and a hopeful outlook on life. They contribute to psychological resilience, helping individuals cope with stress and adversity. For example:

- Self-Worth: Believing in one's worth and capabilities can enhance self-esteem and confidence, leading to proactive behaviors and achievements.

- Trust in Others: Believing in the goodness and reliability of others can foster supportive relationships and social connectedness, which are crucial for mental well-being.

- Optimism: Viewing the world as a place of opportunities and growth can motivate individuals to pursue goals and embrace challenges, enhancing life satisfaction.

Negative Core Beliefs and Mental Health

Maladaptive core beliefs can contribute to various mental health issues by perpetuating negative thought patterns and emotional distress. Common negative core beliefs and their impact include:

- Low Self-Esteem: Beliefs like "I am unworthy" or "I am a failure" can lead to persistent feelings of inadequacy, depression, and anxiety.

- Distrust of Others: Beliefs such as "People are dangerous" or "I cannot trust anyone" can result in social withdrawal, loneliness, and relationship difficulties.

- Pessimism: Believing that "The world is a harsh place" or "Nothing good ever happens" can foster chronic stress, hopelessness, and a lack of motivation.

Cognitive-Behavioral Theory and Core Beliefs

Cognitive-Behavioral Therapy (CBT) is a widely used psychological approach that addresses the interplay between thoughts, emotions, and behaviors. CBT posits that core beliefs are central to cognitive patterns and can be modified to improve mental health.

Cognitive Triad

CBT identifies a cognitive triad of negative thoughts that commonly occur in depression and anxiety: negative views of the self, the world, and the future. These thoughts are rooted in maladaptive core beliefs, which maintain and exacerbate emotional distress.

Automatic Thoughts and Core Beliefs

Core beliefs give rise to automatic thoughts, which are immediate, involuntary thoughts in response to situations. For example, a person with the core belief "I am unlovable" might automatically think "She doesn't like me" when someone does not respond to a message promptly. Recognizing and challenging these automatic thoughts is a key component of CBT.

Cognitive Restructuring

CBT techniques, such as cognitive restructuring, aim to identify, challenge, and modify negative core beliefs. This process involves:

1. Identifying Core Beliefs: Through self-reflection and therapeutic dialogue, individuals uncover the underlying beliefs that drive their thoughts and behaviors.

2. Challenging Core Beliefs: Individuals examine the evidence for and against their core beliefs, considering alternative perspectives and interpretations.

3. Forming New Beliefs: By developing more balanced and realistic beliefs, individuals can shift their cognitive patterns and improve their mental health.

Empirical Research on Core Beliefs and Mental Health

Empirical studies support the link between core beliefs and mental health, demonstrating how interventions targeting core beliefs can lead to significant improvements in psychological well-being.

Depression and Core Beliefs

Research has shown that negative core beliefs, particularly those related to self-worth and helplessness, are strongly associated with depression. Studies indicate that CBT interventions focusing on these beliefs can reduce depressive symptoms and prevent relapse.

Anxiety Disorders and Core Beliefs

Core beliefs about vulnerability, danger, and control are central to anxiety disorders. For example, individuals with generalized anxiety disorder (GAD) often hold beliefs like "I cannot handle uncertainty" or "I must always be in control."

CBT strategies that challenge these beliefs have been effective in reducing anxiety symptoms.

Eating Disorders and Core Beliefs

Eating disorders are frequently linked to core beliefs about body image, self-worth, and control. Cognitive-behavioral interventions that address these underlying beliefs have been shown to improve treatment outcomes and support long-term recovery.

Practical Strategies for Modifying Core Beliefs

Modifying core beliefs requires a commitment to self-awareness, reflection, and practice. Here are some practical strategies to help individuals reshape their core beliefs:

Self-Reflection and Journaling

Keeping a journal can help individuals track their thoughts and identify recurring patterns linked to core beliefs. Reflecting on these patterns can provide insights into how beliefs influence emotions and behaviors.

Challenging Negative Thoughts

Actively questioning negative automatic thoughts and considering alternative interpretations can weaken the hold of maladaptive core beliefs. This involves:

1. Evidence Gathering: Examining the evidence that supports or contradicts the negative thought.

2. Alternative Explanations: Generating more balanced and realistic interpretations of the situation.

3. Behavioral Experiments: Testing new beliefs through actions and observing the outcomes.

Affirmations and Positive Self-Talk

Using positive affirmations and self-talk can reinforce new, healthier core beliefs. Repeating statements like "I am worthy," "I can trust others," and "The world is full of opportunities" can gradually shift cognitive patterns.

Therapeutic Support

Working with a therapist, particularly one trained in CBT, can provide structured guidance and support in identifying and modifying core beliefs. Therapy offers a safe space for exploring deeply held convictions and developing healthier cognitive frameworks.

Biblical Insights on Belief

The Bible offers wisdom on the transformative power of belief and the importance of aligning our thoughts with spiritual truths. Biblical teachings emphasize faith, hope, and love as foundational beliefs that shape our lives.

Faith and Transformation

Philippians 4:13 declares, "I can do all things through Christ who strengthens me." This verse highlights the power of belief in shaping our reality and guiding our actions. Faith, as a positive and hopeful belief, can lead to profound transformation and resilience.

Renewing the Mind

Romans 12:2 encourages believers to "be transformed by the renewing of your mind." This verse underscores the importance of continually examining and renewing our beliefs in light of spiritual wisdom. Aligning our beliefs with God's truth can lead to inner peace and fulfillment.

Guarding the Heart

Proverbs 4:23, "Above all else, guard your heart, for everything you do flows from it," emphasizes the need to protect our inner beliefs and values. This biblical wisdom aligns with psychological insights, highlighting the central role of belief in shaping our character and actions.

Core beliefs are powerful determinants of mental health and behavior, influencing our thoughts, emotions, and actions. By understanding the nature and impact of these beliefs, we can take steps to cultivate healthier cognitive patterns and enhance our well-being. Through self-reflection, cognitive restructuring, and therapeutic support, we can transform negative core beliefs and develop a more positive and resilient mindset.

As we continue our exploration of the influence of beliefs, let us remember the wisdom of biblical teachings and the insights of psychological theories. By aligning our beliefs with spiritual truths and fostering positive cognitive frameworks, we can create a life that reflects our highest aspirations and deepest values.

The Impact of Low Self-Esteem on Thinking Capabilities

Low self-esteem, a pervasive and damaging core belief, can profoundly affect an individual's thinking capabilities. Rooted in negative self-perceptions and beliefs, low self-esteem skews the way people view themselves, others, and the world, leading to a range of cognitive distortions and impairments. This chapter examines how low self-esteem affects thinking capabilities through the lens of biblical wisdom, drawing insights from scripture to understand and counteract its influence.

Understanding Low Self-Esteem

Low self-esteem is characterized by a lack of confidence and a negative self-view. Individuals with low self-esteem often believe they are unworthy, incompetent, or flawed. These beliefs can stem from various sources, including early life experiences, societal pressures, and personal failures.

Cognitive Impacts of Low Self-Esteem

1. Self-Doubt and Indecisiveness: Individuals with low self-esteem often struggle with self-doubt, which undermines their ability to make decisions confidently. This indecisiveness can lead to missed opportunities and chronic stress.

2. Negative Self-Talk: Persistent negative self-talk reinforces low self-esteem, creating a cycle of self-criticism and diminished self-worth. Thoughts like "I'm not good enough" or "I can't do anything right" become ingrained, further weakening cognitive abilities.

3. Cognitive Distortions: Low self-esteem can lead to cognitive distortions such as overgeneralization, where one negative experience is seen as a pattern of failure, and catastrophizing, where minor setbacks are perceived as disastrous. These distorted thoughts can paralyze an individual, preventing them from thinking clearly and rationally.

4. Reduced Cognitive Flexibility: People with low self-esteem may struggle to adapt to new situations or perspectives. This rigidity can hinder problem-solving skills and creativity, as they are less likely to take risks or explore new ideas.

Biblical Insights on Self-Esteem and Thinking

The Bible provides profound wisdom on the value of individuals and the power of beliefs. Understanding our worth through biblical teachings can help counteract low self-esteem and its detrimental effects on thinking.

God's View of Human Worth

The Bible affirms the inherent worth of every individual, created in the image of God. Genesis 1:27 states, "So God created mankind in his own image, in the image of God he created them; male and female he created them." This foundational truth establishes the intrinsic value of every person, regardless of their circumstances or failures.

Renewing the Mind

Romans 12:2 encourages believers to transform their thinking: "Do not conform to the pattern of this world, but be transformed by the renewing of your mind. Then you will be able to test and approve what God's will is—his good, pleasing, and perfect will." Renewing the mind involves replacing negative, worldly beliefs with the truth of God's word, which can significantly improve self-esteem and cognitive function.

Overcoming Fear and Doubt

Isaiah 41:10 offers reassurance against fear and doubt: "So do not fear, for I am with you; do not be dismayed, for I am your God. I will strengthen you and help you; I will uphold you with my righteous right hand." Recognizing God's support and strength can bolster self-confidence, reducing the impact of low self-esteem on thinking capabilities.

The Power of Positive Confession

Proverbs 18:21 highlights the power of words: "The tongue has the power of life and death, and those who love it will eat its fruit." Positive confessions and affirmations based on biblical truths can help rewire negative thought patterns, promoting healthier self-esteem and more effective thinking.

Practical Steps to Improve Self-Esteem and Cognitive Function

To combat the effects of low self-esteem and enhance cognitive capabilities, individuals can take practical steps grounded in both biblical wisdom and psychological principles.

1. Embrace Biblical Truths

Regularly meditate on scriptures that affirm your worth and identity in Christ. Verses like Psalm 139:14, "I praise you because I am fearfully and wonderfully made; your works are wonderful, I know that full well," can reinforce a positive self-image and counteract negative beliefs.

2. Practice Gratitude

Cultivating gratitude can shift focus from perceived deficiencies to the blessings and strengths in one's life. Philippians 4:6-7 advises, "Do not be anxious about anything, but in every situation, by prayer and petition, with thanksgiving, present your requests to God. And the peace of God, which transcends all understanding, will guard your hearts and your minds in Christ Jesus." Gratitude can enhance mental resilience and clarity.

3. Challenge Negative Thoughts

Actively identify and challenge negative thoughts. Replace them with biblical affirmations and positive self-talk. For example, when faced with self-doubt, recall Philippians 4:13, "I can do all things through Christ who strengthens me," to reinforce your capability and worth.

4. Seek Support and Accountability

Engage in supportive communities and seek accountability partners who can offer encouragement and constructive feedback. Ecclesiastes 4:9-10 reminds us, "Two are better than one because they have a good return for their labor: If either of them falls, one can help the other up."

5. Develop a Growth Mindset

Adopt a growth mindset, focusing on learning and personal development rather than fixed traits. James 1:5 encourages seeking wisdom: "If any of you lacks wisdom, you should ask God, who gives generously to all without finding fault, and it will be given to you." Emphasize progress and effort over perfection.

Low self-esteem can significantly impair thinking capabilities, leading to self-doubt, negative self-talk, cognitive distortions, and reduced cognitive flexibility. However, by embracing biblical truths about our worth and identity, practicing gratitude, challenging negative thoughts, seeking support, and developing a growth mindset, we can counteract these effects and enhance our cognitive function.

Biblical wisdom provides a powerful foundation for building healthy self-esteem, transforming our thoughts, and improving our overall mental health. By aligning our beliefs with God's truth and actively working to renew our minds, we can overcome the limitations imposed by low self-esteem and live more fulfilling, effective lives. As Proverbs 23:7 reminds us, "For as he thinks in his heart, so is he," highlighting the profound impact of our beliefs on our reality and destiny.

CHAPTER 04

THE CREATIVE POWER OF THOUGHT

The human mind possesses an extraordinary ability to shape and transform reality through the power of thought. This creative aspect of thought is not merely a philosophical abstraction but a profound truth explored by thinkers throughout history. In this chapter, we will delve into the works of Ralph Waldo Emerson and Friedrich Nietzsche to understand how they conceptualized the creative power of thought and its implications for personal and societal transformation.

Ralph Waldo Emerson: The Transcendental Vision

Ralph Waldo Emerson, a leading figure in the transcendentalist movement, believed deeply in the inherent creative power of the human mind. Emerson's philosophy emphasized the unity of the individual with the universe and the divine, suggesting that through thought, individuals could tap into a greater creative force.

The Oversoul and Individual Creativity

Emerson introduced the concept of the "Oversoul," a universal spirit that connects all beings. According to Emerson, each person is an expression of this divine essence, and through deep introspection and connection with the Oversoul, one can access boundless creative potential. He writes in his essay "The Over-Soul": "We live in succession, in division, in parts, in particles. Meantime within man is the soul of the whole; the wise silence; the universal beauty, to which every part and particle is equally related, the eternal ONE."

This idea suggests that creativity is not merely an individual endeavor but a channeling of the universal creative spirit. By aligning one's thoughts with the divine, one can transcend ordinary limitations and achieve extraordinary creativity.

Self-Reliance and the Power of Thought

In his seminal essay "Self-Reliance," Emerson argues for the importance of trusting oneself and one's thoughts. He believed that self-reliance and individualism are essential for tapping into one's creative potential. Emerson famously wrote, "Trust thyself: every heart vibrates to that iron string." This call to self-trust underscores the belief that each person's thoughts and ideas are powerful and worthy of expression.

Emerson's philosophy encourages individuals to listen to their inner voice and follow their unique path, suggesting that true creativity emerges when one is authentic and self-reliant. By embracing their thoughts and trusting their inner guidance, individuals can manifest their creative visions in the world.

Friedrich Nietzsche: The Will to Power and Creative Transformation

Friedrich Nietzsche, a German philosopher known for his provocative ideas, also explored the creative power of thought, albeit from a different perspective. Nietzsche's concept of the "Will to Power" highlights the dynamic and transformative nature of human thought.

The Will to Power as Creative Force

Nietzsche's "Will to Power" is a fundamental drive inherent in all living beings to assert and enhance their power. He saw this will as the primary force behind all human actions and achievements, including creative endeavors. Nietzsche argued that creativity is an expression of the Will to Power, where individuals seek to overcome obstacles and create new values and realities.

In "Thus Spoke Zarathustra," Nietzsche writes, "What is great in man is that he is a bridge and not a goal: what can be loved in man is that he is an over-going and a down-going." This metaphor of man as a bridge suggests that human beings are always in a state of becoming, driven by their will to create and transform.

Overcoming and Self-Overcoming

Nietzsche believed that true creativity involves overcoming existing limitations and continuously striving for self-improvement. This process of self-overcoming requires critical self-reflection and the courage to challenge conventional beliefs and norms. By doing so, individuals can break free from societal constraints and unleash their creative potential.

In "The Gay Science," Nietzsche declares, "One must still have chaos in oneself to be able to give birth to a dancing star." This statement emphasizes the necessity of embracing inner chaos and complexity as a source of creativity. Rather than seeking order and stability, Nietzsche encourages embracing the dynamic and often tumultuous nature of thought to foster innovation and artistic expression.

The Intersection of Emerson and Nietzsche

While Emerson and Nietzsche approached the concept of creative thought from different angles, their philosophies intersect in several key areas:

1. The Importance of Individualism:

Both Emerson and Nietzsche emphasized the importance of individualism and self-expression. Emerson's call for self-reliance and Nietzsche's focus on the Will to Power both advocate for the empowerment of the individual as the source of creativity.

2. The Transcendent Nature of Thought:

Emerson's belief in the Oversoul and Nietzsche's idea of overcoming suggest that thought has a transcendent quality, enabling individuals to connect with higher truths or greater forces. For Emerson, this connection is divine, while for Nietzsche, it is an assertion of personal power and transformation.

3. The Transformative Power of Creativity:

Both philosophers recognized that creativity is a transformative process. Emerson saw it as a way to align with the universal spirit, while Nietzsche viewed it as a means to continually redefine oneself and the world.

Practical Applications of Creative Thought

Understanding the creative power of thought through the philosophies of Emerson and Nietzsche can inspire practical applications in daily life. Here are some strategies to harness this power:

1. Embrace Authenticity:

Trust in your thoughts and ideas, as Emerson suggests. Authenticity and self-reliance are key to unlocking creative potential. Avoid conforming to external expectations and instead follow your inner voice.

2. Seek Continuous Growth:

Adopt Nietzsche's principle of self-overcoming. Continuously challenge yourself to grow and evolve. Embrace new experiences, learn from failures, and strive to surpass your limitations.

3. Connect with a Higher Purpose:

Find ways to connect your creative endeavors with a higher purpose or vision. Whether through spiritual practices, personal reflection, or alignment with core values, linking your creativity to a greater goal can provide motivation and inspiration.

4. Embrace Complexity and Chaos:

Don't shy away from complexity or chaos. Recognize that the most creative ideas often emerge from periods of uncertainty and confusion. Allow yourself to explore and experiment without fear of failure.

Biblical Reflections on Creative Thought

The Bible also provides insights into the creative power of thought, emphasizing the divine nature of human creativity.

Created in God's Image

Genesis 1:27 states, "So God created mankind in his own image, in the image of God he created them; male and female he created them." This verse highlights that humans are endowed with creative capabilities because they are made in the image of a Creator. Our ability to think and create is a reflection of God's own creativity.

Renewing the Mind

Romans 12:2 again reminds us of the transformative power of thought: "Do not conform to the pattern of this world, but be transformed by the renewing of your mind." By renewing our minds and aligning our thoughts with divine wisdom, we can tap into our creative potential and bring about positive change in our lives and the world around us.

The Power of Words

Proverbs 18:21 underscores the creative power of language and thought: "The tongue has the power of life and death, and those who love it will eat its fruit." Our thoughts and words have the power to shape reality, highlighting the importance of cultivating positive and constructive thoughts.

The creative power of thought, as explored by Emerson and Nietzsche, underscores the profound impact our thinking can have on our reality and destiny. By embracing individuality, seeking continuous growth, connecting with higher purposes, and embracing complexity, we can unlock our creative potential.

Integrating these philosophical insights with biblical wisdom offers a holistic approach to understanding and harnessing the power of thought. As we continue to explore the influence of beliefs and the power of our inner world, let us remember that our thoughts have the potential to shape not only our own lives but also the world around us.

The Role of Visualization and Positive Thinking in Personal Development

The human mind is a powerful tool capable of shaping our reality and influencing our future. In psychology, two key concepts that harness this power are visualization and positive thinking. These techniques are widely recognized for their effectiveness in personal development, enabling individuals to achieve their goals, enhance their well-being, and transform their lives. This chapter explores how visualization and positive thinking work, their psychological underpinnings, and practical applications for personal growth.

The Science of Visualization

Visualization, also known as mental imagery, involves creating vivid and detailed images of desired outcomes in the mind. This technique leverages the brain's ability to simulate real experiences, which can significantly impact one's motivation, confidence, and performance.

How Visualization Works

Visualization activates neural pathways in the brain similar to those used during actual performance. This phenomenon is supported by research in neuroscience, which shows that the brain does not distinguish much between real and imagined experiences. When we visualize, we engage our sensory and motor cortices, effectively 'practicing' the activity mentally.

Studies on Visualization

Numerous studies have demonstrated the effectiveness of visualization in various fields. For example, research on athletes has shown that mental practice through visualization can improve performance nearly as effectively as physical practice. A study conducted by Dr. Biasiotto at the University of Chicago found that basketball players who visualized making free throws improved their shooting accuracy almost as much as those who practiced physically.

Benefits of Visualization

1. Enhanced Performance: By mentally rehearsing actions, individuals can improve their skills and performance in sports, academics, and professional endeavors.

2. Increased Confidence: Visualization helps build self-efficacy, the belief in one's ability to succeed. This confidence can translate into better performance and persistence in the face of challenges.

3. Stress Reduction: Visualizing positive outcomes can reduce anxiety and stress, promoting a more relaxed and focused state of mind.

Positive Thinking and Its Psychological Impact

Positive thinking involves maintaining an optimistic outlook and focusing on favorable outcomes. This mindset can profoundly affect one's mental health, resilience, and overall well-being.

The Power of Positive Thinking

Positive thinking is rooted in cognitive-behavioral theory, which posits that our thoughts influence our emotions and behaviors. By consciously adopting a positive mindset, individuals can alter their emotional responses and behavior patterns, leading to better mental health and improved life outcomes.

Research on Positive Thinking

Extensive research supports the benefits of positive thinking. Dr. Martin Seligman, a pioneer in the field of positive psychology, found that optimistic individuals tend to experience better physical health, lower stress levels, and greater life satisfaction compared to pessimists. His work highlights the connection between a positive mindset and overall well-being.

Benefits of Positive Thinking

1. Improved Mental Health: Positive thinking reduces the risk of depression and anxiety, fostering a more resilient and optimistic outlook on life.

2. Enhanced Problem-Solving: Optimistic individuals are more likely to approach problems with a solution-focused mindset, increasing their ability to overcome obstacles.

3. Better Physical Health: Studies have shown that positive thinking is associated with lower levels of stress hormones, better cardiovascular health, and a stronger immune system.

Integrating Visualization and Positive Thinking

Combining visualization and positive thinking can amplify their benefits, creating a powerful toolset for personal development. Here's how to effectively integrate these techniques:

1. Set Clear Goals

Begin by setting clear, specific, and achievable goals. Whether aiming for career success, academic achievement, or personal growth, having a defined target is crucial. Write down your goals and review them regularly to stay focused and motivated.

2. Practice Daily Visualization

Dedicate time each day to visualize your goals. Find a quiet place, close your eyes, and imagine yourself achieving your desired outcomes in vivid detail. Engage all your senses to make the visualization as realistic as possible. For instance, if your goal is to deliver a successful presentation, visualize the audience's positive reactions, hear the applause, and feel the confidence in your voice.

3. Cultivate Positive Affirmations

Positive affirmations are statements that reinforce optimistic beliefs about yourself and your abilities. Create a list of affirmations related to your goals and repeat them daily. Examples include, "I am capable of achieving my goals," "I am confident and skilled," and "I attract success and positivity."

4. Challenge Negative Thoughts

Recognize and challenge any negative thoughts that arise. Replace them with positive alternatives. For example, if you catch yourself thinking, "I can't do this," reframe it to, "I am fully capable and prepared to succeed." This practice helps to rewire your brain to favor positive thinking patterns.

5. Visualize Overcoming Challenges

Visualization is not just about imagining success; it's also about preparing for obstacles. Visualize potential challenges and mentally rehearse overcoming them. This approach builds resilience and equips you with strategies to handle difficulties when they arise.

6. Maintain a Positive Environment

Surround yourself with positive influences, such as supportive friends, inspirational books, and motivational media. A positive environment reinforces your mindset and keeps you focused on your goals.

The Bible also offers valuable insights into the power of thought and its impact on our lives.

Visualization and Faith

Hebrews 11:1 defines faith as "the substance of things hoped for, the evidence of things not seen." This verse aligns closely with the concept of visualization, emphasizing the importance of believing in and envisioning positive outcomes even before they manifest.

Positive Thinking in Scripture

Philippians 4:8 encourages believers to focus on positive and uplifting thoughts: "Finally, brothers and sisters, whatever is true, whatever is noble, whatever is right, whatever is pure, whatever is lovely, whatever is admirable— if anything is excellent or praiseworthy—think about such things." This directive underscores the importance of maintaining a positive mindset.

Strength and Encouragement

Isaiah 41:10 offers reassurance and strength: "So do not fear, for I am with you; do not be dismayed, for I am your God. I will strengthen you and help you; I will uphold you with my righteous right hand." Believing in God's support and visualizing His guidance can enhance confidence and reduce anxiety.

Visualization and positive thinking are powerful tools for personal development, supported by both psychological research and biblical wisdom. By harnessing the creative power of thought, individuals can transform their lives, achieve their goals, and enhance their overall well-being. Integrating these techniques into daily practice can lead to profound and lasting changes, empowering individuals to create the life they envision.

The human mind is an extraordinary instrument capable of shaping and transforming reality through the power of thought. In this chapter, we delve into the concept of creative thought, exploring its profound impact on personal development and achievement. Drawing insights from psychology and the Bible, we will understand how visualization and positive thinking can unlock our potential and lead to a more fulfilling life. The verse from Ephesians 3:20 reminds us of the boundless possibilities that lie within us, empowered by a higher force.

The Role of Visualization and Positive Thinking in Personal Development

The Science of Visualization

Visualization, or mental imagery, involves creating detailed images of desired outcomes in the mind. This technique leverages the brain's ability to simulate real experiences, significantly impacting motivation, confidence, and performance.

How Visualization Works

Visualization activates neural pathways in the brain similar to those used during actual performance. Neuroscience research shows that the brain does not distinguish much between real and imagined experiences. When we visualize, we engage our sensory and motor cortices, effectively 'practicing' the activity mentally.

Studies on Visualization

Numerous studies have demonstrated the effectiveness of visualization. For instance, research on athletes has shown that mental practice through visualization can improve performance nearly as effectively as physical practice. A study conducted by Dr. Biasiotto at the University of Chicago found that basketball players who visualized making free throws improved their shooting accuracy almost as much as those who practiced physically.

Benefits of Visualization

1. Enhanced Performance: Mental rehearsal improves skills and performance in various fields, including sports, academics, and professional endeavors.

2. Increased Confidence: Visualization helps build self-efficacy, the belief in one's ability to succeed, translating into better performance and persistence.

3. Stress Reduction: Visualizing positive outcomes reduces anxiety and stress, promoting a more relaxed and focused state of mind.

Positive thinking involves maintaining an optimistic outlook and focusing on favorable outcomes. This mindset can profoundly affect mental health, resilience, and overall well-being.

The Power of Positive Thinking

Positive thinking is rooted in cognitive-behavioral theory, which posits that our thoughts influence our emotions and behaviors. By consciously adopting a positive mindset, individuals can alter their emotional responses and behavior patterns, leading to better mental health and improved life outcomes.

Research on Positive Thinking

Extensive research supports the benefits of positive thinking. Dr. Martin Seligman, a pioneer in positive psychology, found that optimistic individuals experience better physical health, lower stress levels, and greater life satisfaction compared to pessimists. His work highlights the connection between a positive mindset and overall well-being.

Benefits of Positive Thinking

1. Improved Mental Health: Positive thinking reduces the risk of depression and anxiety, fostering a more resilient and optimistic outlook.

2. Enhanced Problem-Solving: Optimistic individuals approach problems with a solution-focused mindset, increasing their ability to overcome obstacles.

3. Better Physical Health: Positive thinking is associated with lower stress hormones, better cardiovascular health, and a stronger immune system.

Integrating Visualization and Positive Thinking

Combining visualization and positive thinking can amplify their benefits, creating a powerful toolset for personal development. Here's how to effectively integrate these techniques:

1. Set Clear Goals

Begin by setting clear, specific, and achievable goals. Whether aiming for career success, academic achievement, or personal growth, having a defined target is crucial. Write down your goals and review them regularly to stay focused and motivated.

2. Practice Daily Visualization

Dedicate time each day to visualize your goals. Find a quiet place, close your eyes, and imagine yourself achieving your desired outcomes in vivid detail. Engage all your senses to make the visualization as realistic as possible. For instance, if your goal is to deliver a successful presentation, visualize the audience's positive reactions, hear the applause, and feel the confidence in your voice.

3. Cultivate Positive Affirmations

Positive affirmations are statements that reinforce optimistic beliefs about yourself and your abilities. Create a list of affirmations related to your goals and repeat them daily. Examples include, "I am capable of achieving my goals," "I am confident and skilled," and "I attract success and positivity."

4. Challenge Negative Thoughts

Recognize and challenge any negative thoughts that arise. Replace them with positive alternatives. For example, if you catch yourself thinking, "I can't do this," reframe it to, "I am fully capable and prepared to succeed." This practice helps to rewire your brain to favor positive thinking patterns.

5. Visualize Overcoming Challenges

Visualization is not just about imagining success; it's also about preparing for obstacles. Visualize potential challenges and mentally rehearse overcoming them. This approach builds resilience and equips you with strategies to handle difficulties when they arise.

6. Maintain a Positive Environment

Surround yourself with positive influences, such as supportive friends, inspirational books, and motivational media. A positive environment reinforces your mindset and keeps you focused on your goals.

Biblical Insights on Creative Thought

The Bible provides profound insights into the power of thought and its creative potential. Ephesians 3:20 states, "Now to him who is able to do immeasurably more than all we ask or imagine, according to his power that is at work within us." This verse highlights the limitless possibilities when we harness the power of our thoughts through faith and divine guidance.

Created in God's Image

Genesis 1:27 reminds us that we are created in God's image, endowed with creative capabilities: "So God created mankind in his own image, in the image of God he created them; male and female he created them." Our ability to think and create reflects the divine creativity inherent in us.

Renewing the Mind

Romans 12:2 emphasizes the transformative power of thought: "Do not conform to the pattern of this world, but be transformed by the renewing of your mind." By renewing our minds and aligning our thoughts with divine wisdom, we can unlock our creative potential and bring about positive change.

The Power of Words

Proverbs 18:21 underscores the creative power of language and thought: "The tongue has the power of life and death, and those who love it will eat its fruit." Our thoughts and words shape our reality, highlighting the importance of cultivating positive and constructive thoughts.

Practical Applications of Creative Thought

Understanding the creative power of thought can inspire practical applications in daily life. Here are some strategies to harness this power:

1. Embrace Authenticity:

Trust in your thoughts and ideas. Authenticity and self-reliance are key to unlocking creative potential. Avoid conforming to external expectations and follow your inner voice.

2. Seek Continuous Growth:

Adopt a principle of self-overcoming. Continuously challenge yourself to grow and evolve. Embrace new experiences, learn from failures, and strive to surpass your limitations.

3. Connect with a Higher Purpose:

Find ways to connect your creative endeavors with a higher purpose or vision. Whether through spiritual practices, personal reflection, or alignment with core values, linking your creativity to a greater goal can provide motivation and inspiration.

4. Embrace Complexity and Chaos:

Don't shy away from complexity or chaos. Recognize that the most creative ideas often emerge from periods of uncertainty and confusion. Allow yourself to explore and experiment without fear of failure.

The creative power of thought, supported by psychological research and biblical wisdom, highlights the profound impact our thinking can have on our reality and destiny. By embracing visualization, positive thinking, and the principles outlined in scripture, we can unlock our potential and transform our lives. As Ephesians 3:20 reminds us, the possibilities are immeasurable when we align our thoughts with divine power. Let us harness this creative power to shape a brighter and more fulfilling future.

94

CHAPTER 05

THOUGHTS AND CHARACTER

The relationship between thoughts and character has been a subject of profound interest across various philosophical traditions. Two towering figures in this discourse are Aristotle and Confucius, whose insights provide a comprehensive understanding of how our internal thoughts mold our external character. This chapter delves into their teachings, exploring the intricate connection between thought and character formation.

Aristotle's Perspective on Thoughts and Character

The Role of Virtue

Aristotle, one of the most influential philosophers in Western thought, posited that character is fundamentally shaped by our thoughts and actions. In his seminal work, Nicomachean Ethics, Aristotle introduces the concept of virtue ethics, emphasizing that virtuous character is developed through the habitual practice of virtuous actions. He asserts that virtues are dispositions cultivated by consistent, thoughtful actions.

Thoughts as Seeds of Action

According to Aristotle, our thoughts are the seeds from which our actions grow. Every action we take is preceded by a thought, which implies that the quality of our thoughts directly influences the quality of our actions. If our thoughts are aligned with virtues such as courage, temperance, and wisdom, our actions will naturally reflect these virtues, shaping our character positively.

The Doctrine of the Mean

Aristotle's doctrine of the mean further elucidates the connection between thought and character. He argues that virtue lies in finding a balance between excess and deficiency, a balance achieved through rational thought. For example, courage is a mean between recklessness and cowardice, and it is through thoughtful deliberation that one can navigate this balance.

Habit and Character Formation

Aristotle famously stated, "We are what we repeatedly do. Excellence, then, is not an act, but a habit." This highlights the importance of habitual thought and action in character formation. By consistently engaging in virtuous thoughts and actions, we develop a virtuous character, which becomes an integral part of our identity.

Confucius on Thoughts and Character

The Centrality of Virtue

Confucius, a preeminent philosopher in Eastern thought, similarly emphasized the centrality of virtue in character formation. His teachings, primarily recorded in the Analects, focus on the cultivation of virtues such as benevolence (ren), righteousness (yi), propriety (li), and wisdom (zhi). For Confucius, these virtues are not only outward behaviors but also inward dispositions shaped by thoughtful reflection and self-cultivation.

The Role of Reflection

Confucius placed significant importance on reflection as a means of character development. He believed that individuals must continuously reflect on their thoughts and actions to ensure they align with virtuous principles. This process of introspection helps individuals recognize and correct their flaws, leading to the cultivation of a noble character.

The Influence of Thoughts on Actions

In Confucian philosophy, thoughts are seen as the precursors to actions. Confucius taught that righteous thoughts lead to righteous actions, which in turn shape a person's character. He emphasized the importance of sincerity and authenticity in one's thoughts, as insincere thoughts could not lead to genuine virtuous actions.

The Role of Rituals and Social Harmony

Confucius also highlighted the role of rituals (li) in shaping character. He believed that participating in rituals with sincere and thoughtful intention helps cultivate virtues and reinforces social harmony. These rituals serve as a means of aligning one's thoughts and actions with communal and ethical standards, thus shaping a virtuous character.

Integrating Aristotle and Confucius: Thoughts and Character in Practice

While Aristotle and Confucius come from different cultural backgrounds, their teachings converge on the idea that thoughts play a critical role in shaping character. Both philosophers emphasize the importance of habitual practice and reflection in developing virtuous character.

Practical Steps for Character Development

1. Cultivate Virtuous Thoughts:

Regularly engage in reflective practices that encourage virtuous thinking. This can include journaling, meditation, or contemplation on ethical principles.

2. Practice Habitual Actions:

Implement consistent actions that reflect virtuous thoughts. Start with small, daily habits that align with virtues such as kindness, honesty, and diligence.

3. Engage in Reflection:

Dedicate time for introspection to assess whether your thoughts and actions are in harmony with your ethical values. Use this reflection to make necessary adjustments and improvements.

4. Participate in Community Rituals:

Engage in rituals or practices that reinforce virtuous behavior and social harmony. This can include community service, religious observances, or family traditions that promote ethical living.

5. Seek Balance:

Strive to find the mean between extremes in your thoughts and actions. Use rational deliberation to navigate the complexities of ethical decisions, aiming for balanced and moderate responses.

Biblical Insights on Thoughts and Character

The Bible also offers profound insights into the relationship between thoughts and character. Proverbs 23:7 states, "For as he thinks in his heart, so is he." This verse underscores the significance of our inner thoughts in defining who we are.

Guarding the Heart and Mind

Proverbs 4:23 advises, "Above all else, guard your heart, for everything you do flows from it." This highlights the importance of guarding our thoughts and ensuring they are aligned with virtuous and righteous principles.

Transformation through Renewal

Romans 12:2 encourages believers to transform their character through the renewal of their minds: "Do not conform to the pattern of this world, but be transformed by the renewing of your mind." By renewing our thoughts with divine wisdom, we can cultivate a character that reflects godly virtues.

The teachings of Aristotle and Confucius provide a comprehensive understanding of how our thoughts shape our character. By cultivating virtuous thoughts, practicing habitual actions, and engaging in reflective practices, we can develop a noble character that aligns with ethical principles. The biblical perspective reinforces this connection, emphasizing the importance of guarding our thoughts and renewing our minds to transform our character. Through these combined insights, we can harness the creative power of thought to shape a virtuous and fulfilling life.

The intricate relationship between thoughts and character has long been a subject of fascination for philosophers and psychologists alike. This chapter explores how habitual thoughts and behaviors contribute to the development of character from a psychological perspective. By examining theories and research on habit formation and the influence of cognitive patterns on behavior, we can gain a deeper understanding of the mechanisms through which character is shaped.

The Psychology of Habitual Thoughts and Behaviors

Habit Formation and Character

Understanding Habits

Habits are automatic responses to specific cues, developed through repeated practice. They represent a significant portion of our daily actions and play a crucial role in shaping our character. According to psychologist William James, habits are the "flywheel of society," driving much of our behavior. The formation of habits involves a three-step process known as the habit loop: cue, routine, and reward.

1. Cue: The trigger that initiates the habit.

2. Routine: The behavior performed in response to the cue.

3. Reward: The positive outcome that reinforces the habit.

Research on Habit Formation

Studies have shown that habits are formed through consistent repetition. Research by Lally et al. (2010) suggests that, on average, it takes about 66 days to form a new habit. The study also found that the complexity of the behavior influences the time required for habit formation; simpler habits are established more quickly than complex ones.

Impact of Habits on Character

Habits play a critical role in shaping character because they reflect and reinforce our underlying thoughts and values. When we repeatedly engage in behaviors that align with virtues such as honesty, kindness, and diligence, these actions become ingrained in our character. Conversely, negative habits can undermine our character and lead to detrimental outcomes.

Cognitive Patterns and Character Development

The Role of Cognitive Schemas

Cognitive schemas are mental frameworks that help us organize and interpret information. They influence our perceptions, thoughts, and behaviors. Schemas are developed through our experiences and shape our understanding of the world. For example, a person with a schema that emphasizes trustworthiness will likely engage in behaviors that reflect honesty and integrity.

Automatic Thoughts and Behavior

Automatic thoughts are spontaneous, involuntary thoughts that arise in response to specific situations. These thoughts are often shaped by our cognitive schemas and can significantly influence our behavior. According to cognitive-behavioral theory, automatic thoughts can be positive or negative and play a crucial role in shaping our emotional and behavioral responses.

Self-Perception and Character

Our self-perception, or the way we view ourselves, is a key determinant of our behavior and character development. Positive self-perception can lead to constructive behaviors and the cultivation of virtues, while negative self-perception can result in harmful behaviors and character flaws. Research by Markus and Nurius (1986) on the concept of possible selves highlights how our beliefs about who we can become influence our motivation and actions.

Practical Strategies for Developing Virtuous Character

Understanding the psychological mechanisms behind habitual thoughts and behaviors can inform practical strategies for character development. Here are some approaches to cultivating virtuous character through the power of thought and habit:

1. Identify and Modify Negative Habits

The first step in character development is identifying negative habits that undermine your desired character traits. Use self-reflection and mindfulness to recognize these habits and their triggers. Once identified, work on modifying these habits by replacing them with positive alternatives. For example, if procrastination is a negative habit, replace it with a habit of setting specific goals and deadlines.

2. Develop Positive Cognitive Schemas

Cultivating positive cognitive schemas involves challenging and reframing negative beliefs and thought patterns. Cognitive-behavioral techniques such as cognitive restructuring can help you identify irrational or harmful thoughts and replace them with rational and constructive ones. For instance, if you have a schema that leads to self-doubt, practice affirmations and evidence-based thinking to build self-confidence.

3. Establish Virtuous Routines

Create routines that reinforce virtuous behaviors. Start with small, manageable actions that align with your desired character traits. Consistency is key to habit formation, so incorporate these routines into your daily life. For example, if kindness is a desired virtue, make it a habit to perform one act of kindness each day, whether it's complimenting a colleague or helping a neighbor.

4. Utilize Goal Setting and Self-Monitoring

Goal setting is a powerful tool for character development. Set specific, measurable, achievable, relevant, and time-bound (SMART) goals that align with your character aspirations. Regularly monitor your progress and adjust your goals as needed. Self-monitoring techniques such as journaling can help you track your thoughts, behaviors, and achievements, providing valuable insights into your character development journey.

5. Practice Mindfulness and Self-Reflection

Mindfulness and self-reflection are essential practices for cultivating self-awareness and intentionality in your thoughts and actions. Mindfulness involves paying attention to the present moment without judgment, helping you become more aware of your automatic thoughts and habitual behaviors. Self-reflection allows you to evaluate your actions and their alignment with your values, facilitating continuous character growth.

6. Seek Social Support and Accountability

Social support and accountability can significantly enhance your efforts to develop virtuous character. Surround yourself with individuals who share your values and can provide encouragement and constructive feedback. Consider joining a group or finding a mentor who can offer guidance and hold you accountable for your character development goals.

The Bible offers profound insights into the relationship between thoughts and character, emphasizing the transformative power of renewing the mind. Proverbs 23:7 states, "For as he thinks in his heart, so is he," highlighting the impact of our internal thoughts on our external character.

Renewing the Mind

Romans 12:2 encourages believers to transform their character through the renewal of their minds: "Do not conform to the pattern of this world, but be transformed by the renewing of your mind." This renewal involves aligning our thoughts with divine wisdom and cultivating virtues such as love, humility, and patience.

Guarding the Heart

Proverbs 4:23 advises, "Above all else, guard your heart, for everything you do flows from it." This verse underscores the importance of protecting our thoughts and ensuring they are aligned with virtuous principles, as our actions and character flow from our inner thoughts.

The development of character through habitual thoughts and behaviors is a dynamic process influenced by cognitive patterns and repeated actions. By understanding the psychological mechanisms behind habit formation and cognitive schemas, we can cultivate a virtuous character that aligns with our values and aspirations. The biblical perspective reinforces the importance of renewing our minds and guarding our thoughts, guiding us toward a life of integrity and virtue. Through intentional effort and practice, we can harness the power of our thoughts to shape a noble and fulfilling character.

The interplay between thoughts and character is a profound and intricate relationship that shapes the essence of who we are. This chapter explores how our habitual thoughts and behaviors contribute to character development, drawing insights from both psychology and biblical wisdom. The verse from Romans 12:2, "Do not be conformed to this world, but be transformed by the renewal of your mind," serves as a guiding principle for understanding the transformative power of thought.

Habitual Thoughts and Character Formation

The Psychology of Habitual Thoughts

The Role of Habits in Character Development

Habits are automatic behaviors triggered by specific cues, which are reinforced by rewards. They form a significant part of our daily routines and play a crucial role in character development. According to Charles Duhigg, author of The Power of Habit, habits shape our lives by creating predictable patterns of behavior. Over time, these patterns become integral to our character.

Mechanisms of Habit Formation

The process of habit formation involves three primary components:

1. Cue: A trigger that initiates the habit.

2. Routine: The behavior itself.

3. Reward: The positive reinforcement that solidifies the habit.

Research by Phillippa Lally and colleagues (2010) indicates that it takes an average of 66 days to form a new habit, with some variations depending on the complexity of the behavior. The consistent repetition of these behaviors gradually shapes our character.

Cognitive Schemas and Automatic Thoughts

Cognitive schemas are mental structures that help us organize and interpret information. These schemas influence our automatic thoughts, which are spontaneous and often subconscious responses to our environment. According to cognitive-behavioral theory, our automatic thoughts play a crucial role in shaping our emotional and behavioral responses. Positive schemas lead to constructive thoughts and behaviors, while negative schemas can result in detrimental patterns.

Self-Perception and Behavior

Our self-perception, or the way we view ourselves, is a critical determinant of our behavior and character. The concept of possible selves, as explored by Markus and Nurius (1986), suggests that our beliefs about who we can become influence our motivation and actions. Positive self-perception encourages virtuous behavior and character development, while negative self-perception can hinder growth and lead to character flaws.

Biblical Perspective on Thought and Character

The Bible offers profound insights into the relationship between thoughts and character. Romans 12:2 emphasizes the importance of renewing our minds to transform our character: "Do not be conformed to this world, but be transformed by the renewal of your mind." This verse underscores the need to align our thoughts with divine wisdom to cultivate a virtuous character.

Renewing the Mind

Renewing the mind involves a deliberate effort to shift our thoughts from worldly influences to godly principles. This transformation is essential for character development, as our thoughts influence our actions and, ultimately, our character. The process of renewing the mind includes:

1. Reflection on Scripture: Meditating on biblical teachings to align our thoughts with God's wisdom.

2. Prayer and Contemplation: Seeking divine guidance to transform our mindset and behaviors.

3. Positive Affirmations: Replacing negative thoughts with affirmations rooted in biblical truths.

Guarding the Heart

Proverbs 4:23 advises, "Above all else, guard your heart, for everything you do flows from it." This verse highlights the importance of protecting our thoughts, as they are the wellspring of our actions. Guarding our hearts involves:

1. Mindful Awareness: Being conscious of the thoughts we entertain and their impact on our behavior.

2. Filtering Influences: Choosing to engage with positive, uplifting content that reinforces virtuous thoughts.

3. Cultivating Gratitude: Focusing on gratitude to foster positive thinking and a resilient character.

Practical Strategies for Character Development

Understanding the psychological and biblical principles behind thought and character can inform practical strategies for personal growth. Here are some approaches to cultivating a virtuous character:

1. Identify and Modify Negative Habits

Recognize negative habits that undermine your character and work on replacing them with positive alternatives. For instance, if you struggle with procrastination, develop a habit of setting specific goals and deadlines.

2. Develop Positive Cognitive Schemas

Challenge and reframe negative beliefs through cognitive restructuring. Practice affirmations and evidence-based thinking to build a positive self-perception.

3. Establish Virtuous Routines

Create daily routines that reinforce virtuous behaviors. Consistency in practicing small, positive actions can lead to significant character development over time.

4. Engage in Regular Reflection

Dedicate time for self-reflection to assess whether your thoughts and actions align with your values. Use tools like journaling to track your progress and make necessary adjustments.

5. Seek Social Support and Accountability

Surround yourself with individuals who share your values and can provide encouragement and constructive feedback. Consider joining a group or finding a mentor for guidance and accountability.

The Transformative Power of Thought

The concept of renewing the mind, as emphasized in Romans 12:2, speaks to the transformative power of thought. By consciously aligning our thoughts with virtuous principles, we can transform our character and live a life that reflects our highest values. The process of character development is ongoing and requires intentional effort, but the rewards are profound.

Thoughts and character are inextricably linked, shaping the essence of who we are. The psychological mechanisms of habit formation and cognitive schemas provide insights into how our thoughts influence our behavior and character. Biblical teachings, particularly the principle of renewing the mind, offer timeless wisdom for cultivating a virtuous character. By understanding and applying these principles, we can harness the power of thought to shape a noble and fulfilling life, transforming ourselves in alignment with our highest values and divine guidance.

The battle between thoughts and character is a profound internal struggle that shapes our moral fiber and spiritual journey. This chapter delves into the dynamic interplay between our mental landscape and our character, drawing on biblical wisdom to understand how we can navigate this battle effectively. By examining key Bible verses, we gain insights into the transformative power of thoughts and the impact they have on our character.

The Nature of the Battle

The conflict between our thoughts and character is an age-old struggle, often described as a battle between the flesh and the spirit. This internal conflict is vividly illustrated in Romans 7:19, where the Apostle Paul writes, "For I do not do the good I want to do, but the evil I do not want to do—this I keep on doing." This verse highlights the tension between our intentions and our actions, a struggle that many of us can relate to.

The Influence of Thoughts on Character

Guarding the Mind

Proverbs 4:23 advises, "Above all else, guard your heart, for everything you do flows from it." The heart, in biblical terms, often represents the seat of our thoughts and emotions. Guarding our heart involves protecting our mind from negative influences and ensuring that our thoughts align with virtuous principles. This proactive approach is essential for developing a character that reflects our highest values.

Renewing the Mind

Romans 12:2 encourages believers to transform their character by renewing their minds: "Do not be conformed to this world, but be transformed by the renewal of your mind."

This renewal involves a conscious effort to replace worldly thoughts with godly ones, aligning our mental patterns with divine wisdom. The process of renewing the mind is a crucial aspect of the battle between thoughts and character, as it helps us cultivate virtues and resist negative influences.

Biblical Examples of the Battle

Jesus in the Wilderness

One of the most profound examples of the battle between thoughts and character is Jesus' temptation in the wilderness, described in Matthew 4:1-11. Jesus faced three temptations that targeted his physical needs, pride, and desire for power. Each time, he countered the temptations with Scripture, demonstrating the power of divine truth in overcoming negative thoughts and maintaining a virtuous character. This narrative illustrates the importance of grounding our thoughts in biblical wisdom to withstand internal and external challenges.

David and Bathsheba

The story of David and Bathsheba, found in 2 Samuel 11, provides a contrasting example of the consequences when thoughts are not aligned with godly principles. David's lustful thoughts led to adultery and subsequent actions that deeply marred his character. This story serves as a cautionary tale, emphasizing the importance of vigilance over our thoughts and the devastating impact they can have on our character if left unchecked.

Practical Strategies for Winning the Battle

1. Scripture Meditation

Meditating on Scripture is a powerful way to align our thoughts with God's wisdom. Psalm 1:2 describes the blessed man as one whose "delight is in the law of the Lord, and on his law he meditates day and night." Regular meditation on biblical truths helps to reinforce positive thought patterns and fortify our character against negative influences.

2. Prayer and Reflection

Prayer is a vital practice for seeking divine guidance in the battle between thoughts and character. Philippians 4:6-7 encourages believers to present their requests to God through prayer and petition, promising that "the peace of God, which transcends all understanding, will guard your hearts and your minds in Christ Jesus." Regular prayer and reflection help us to remain connected to God's will and maintain a virtuous character.

3. Accountability and Community

Engaging with a supportive community provides accountability and encouragement in our spiritual journey. Proverbs 27:17 states, "As iron sharpens iron, so one person sharpens another." Surrounding ourselves with individuals who share our values can help us stay vigilant over our thoughts and actions, promoting character growth through mutual support and accountability.

4. Mindfulness and Self-Awareness

Developing mindfulness and self-awareness allows us to recognize and address negative thoughts before they influence our behavior. 2 Corinthians 10:5 advises believers to "take captive every thought to make it obedient to Christ." By practicing mindfulness, we can identify harmful thoughts and redirect them in alignment with biblical principles, fostering a character that reflects our faith.

5. Positive Affirmations

Using positive affirmations rooted in Scripture can help to reinforce our desired character traits. For example, affirming "I can do all things through Christ who strengthens me" (Philippians 4:13) can bolster our confidence and resilience in the face of challenges. These affirmations serve as reminders of God's promises and our identity in Christ, empowering us to overcome negative thoughts and cultivate a virtuous character.

The Role of the Holy Spirit

The Holy Spirit plays a crucial role in the battle between thoughts and character, providing guidance, conviction, and empowerment. Galatians 5:22-23 describes the fruit of the Spirit as love, joy, peace, forbearance, kindness, goodness, faithfulness, gentleness, and self-control. These qualities are the hallmarks of a character transformed by the Spirit. By yielding to the Holy Spirit's influence, we can experience victory in the battle over our thoughts and develop a character that glorifies God.

The battle between thoughts and character is an ongoing struggle that requires vigilance, intentionality, and divine assistance. By grounding our thoughts in biblical wisdom, practicing mindfulness, and seeking the Holy Spirit's guidance, we can overcome negative influences and cultivate a virtuous character. The transformative power of renewing our minds, as highlighted in Romans 12:2, underscores the significance of aligning our thoughts with God's will. Through diligent effort and reliance on divine strength, we can navigate this internal battle and emerge with a character that reflects our highest values and deepest convictions.

CHAPTER 06

THOUGHT AND CIRCUMSTANCES

The relationship between our thoughts and the circumstances of our lives has been a subject of philosophical inquiry for centuries. Among the many philosophical traditions that have explored this theme, Stoicism offers profound insights into how our internal world shapes our external reality. This chapter delves into the Stoic perspective on the influence of thoughts on circumstances, highlighting the enduring wisdom of this ancient philosophy.

The Stoic Perspective on Thoughts and Circumstances

Foundations of Stoicism

Stoicism, founded in Athens by Zeno of Citium around 300 BCE, teaches that the path to a virtuous and contented life lies in understanding and accepting the natural order of the world. The Stoics believed that while we cannot control external events, we can control our responses to them. This distinction between what is within our control and what is not is central to Stoic philosophy.

The Dichotomy of Control

Epictetus, a prominent Stoic philosopher, articulated the dichotomy of control in his work, the Enchiridion: "Some things are up to us and some things are not." According to Epictetus, our thoughts, beliefs, and attitudes are within our control, whereas external events and other people's actions are not. By focusing on what we can control—our thoughts and reactions—we can maintain inner tranquility regardless of external circumstances.

The Power of Perception

The Stoics emphasized the power of perception in shaping our experience of circumstances. Marcus Aurelius, the Roman Emperor and Stoic philosopher, wrote in his Meditations: "If you are pained by any external thing, it is not this thing that disturbs you, but your judgment about it. And it is in your power to wipe out this judgment now." This teaching underscores the idea that our interpretation of events, rather than the events themselves, determines our emotional response and overall well-being.

Mindfulness and Rationality

Stoicism advocates for mindfulness and rationality as tools for managing thoughts and circumstances. By cultivating awareness of our thoughts and examining them through the lens of reason, we can align our perceptions with reality and respond to situations with wisdom and equanimity. This practice of mindful rationality helps to reduce unnecessary suffering and fosters resilience in the face of life's challenges.

Practical Applications of Stoic Principles

1. Reframing Thoughts

One practical Stoic technique is cognitive reframing—changing the way we think about a situation to alter its emotional impact. For instance, if faced with a difficult challenge, a Stoic might view it as an opportunity for growth and self-improvement rather than a setback. This shift in perspective can transform how we experience and respond to circumstances.

2. Negative Visualization

Negative visualization, or premeditatio malorum, involves contemplating potential negative outcomes to prepare the mind for adversity. By imagining the worst-case scenarios, we can diminish their impact and appreciate the present moment. This Stoic practice helps build mental resilience and reduces anxiety about the future.

3. Acceptance and Commitment

Stoicism teaches the importance of accepting what we cannot change and committing to what we can. This principle is reflected in the Serenity Prayer: "God, grant me the serenity to accept the things I cannot change, courage to change the things I can, and wisdom to know the difference." By embracing acceptance and commitment, we can navigate life's uncertainties with grace and determination.

The Impact of Stoic Thought on Circumstances

Transforming Adversity into Opportunity

The Stoic approach to adversity involves seeing challenges as opportunities for growth and virtue. This mindset shift can transform difficult circumstances into meaningful experiences that contribute to personal development. As Marcus Aurelius observed, "The impediment to action advances action. What stands in the way becomes the way." By embracing obstacles as stepping stones, we can turn adversity into a catalyst for positive change.

Maintaining Inner Peace Amid External Turmoil

Stoicism equips us with tools to maintain inner peace despite external turmoil. By focusing on our internal responses and aligning our thoughts with reason, we can cultivate a sense of calm and stability. This inner peace is not dependent on external conditions but arises from our ability to manage our thoughts and perceptions.

Building Resilience and Fortitude

The Stoic emphasis on rationality and mindfulness fosters resilience and fortitude. By practicing mental discipline and cultivating a balanced perspective, we become better equipped to handle life's challenges with composure and strength. This resilience enables us to persevere through difficult times and emerge stronger.

Biblical Parallels to Stoic Thought

Contentment in All Circumstances

The Apostle Paul echoes Stoic principles in Philippians 4:11-13: "I have learned to be content whatever the circumstances. I know what it is to be in need, and I know what it is to have plenty. I have learned the secret of being content in any and every situation... I can do all this through him who gives me strength." Paul's teachings align with the Stoic idea of finding contentment through internal mastery rather than external conditions.

Renewal of the Mind

Romans 12:2 advises, "Do not conform to the pattern of this world, but be transformed by the renewing of your mind." This call to renew the mind resonates with the Stoic practice of rationally examining and reframing thoughts. By transforming our mindset, we can align our perceptions with higher truths and cultivate a virtuous character.

Trusting in Divine Providence

The Stoic belief in accepting the natural order of the world parallels the biblical teaching of trusting in divine providence. Proverbs 3:5-6 encourages believers to "Trust in the Lord with all your heart and lean not on your own understanding; in all your ways submit to him, and he will make your paths straight." This trust in a higher power provides a foundation for navigating life's uncertainties with faith and serenity.

The Stoic perspective on thoughts and circumstances offers timeless wisdom for navigating the complexities of life. By recognizing the power of our perceptions and focusing on what we can control, we can transform our experiences and cultivate a resilient, virtuous character. The practical applications of Stoic principles, such as cognitive reframing, negative visualization, and acceptance, provide valuable tools for managing thoughts and circumstances effectively.

The parallels between Stoic thought and biblical teachings further enrich our understanding of how to align our internal world with higher principles. By renewing our minds and trusting in divine providence, we can navigate the battle between thoughts and circumstances with grace and wisdom. Ultimately, the integration of Stoic philosophy and biblical wisdom empowers us to live with purpose, resilience, and inner peace, regardless of external conditions.

The concept of "thought and circumstances" delves into how our internal beliefs and perceptions shape the reality we experience. In the realm of psychology, one of the most influential theories that examine this relationship is the concept of locus of control. This chapter explores the psychological implications of locus of control, illustrating how our perception of control over events influences our thoughts, emotions, and behaviors.

The Concept of Locus of Control

Definition and Origins

Locus of control, a concept developed by psychologist Julian B. Rotter in the 1950s, refers to an individual's belief system regarding the causes of their experiences and the factors that influence their life outcomes. It is divided into two primary types: internal locus of control and external locus of control.

Internal Locus of Control

Individuals with an internal locus of control believe that their actions and decisions directly influence the outcomes in their lives. They perceive themselves as the primary agents of change and feel a sense of personal responsibility for their successes and failures. This belief system is associated with higher levels of self-efficacy, motivation, and resilience.

External Locus of Control

Conversely, individuals with an external locus of control believe that external factors—such as luck, fate, or the actions of others—primarily dictate the outcomes in their lives. They perceive themselves as relatively powerless to influence events and often attribute their experiences to forces beyond their control. This belief system is associated with feelings of helplessness, lower self-esteem, and increased stress.

Psychological Implications of Locus of Control

Impact on Mental Health

The locus of control significantly influences mental health. Research has shown that individuals with an internal locus of control tend to experience lower levels of anxiety and depression. They are more likely to engage in proactive coping strategies and feel empowered to manage stress. In contrast, those with an external locus of control may experience higher levels of psychological distress due to their perceived lack of control over life events.

Behavioral Outcomes

The locus of control affects behavior in various contexts, including education, work, and relationships. Individuals with an internal locus of control are more likely to set goals, persist in the face of challenges, and take initiative. Their belief in their ability to influence outcomes fosters a sense of agency and accountability. Conversely, those with an external locus of control may exhibit passivity, avoidance behaviors, and a reluctance to take responsibility for their actions.

Self-Efficacy and Achievement

Self-efficacy, the belief in one's ability to succeed in specific situations, is closely related to locus of control. An internal locus of control enhances self-efficacy, as individuals believe their efforts will lead to desired outcomes. This increased self-efficacy contributes to higher levels of achievement and performance across various domains. On the other hand, an external locus of control can undermine self-efficacy, leading to lower levels of motivation and achievement.

Resilience and Adaptability

Resilience, the ability to bounce back from adversity, is also influenced by locus of control. Those with an internal locus of control are more likely to view challenges as opportunities for growth and learning. Their belief in their ability to influence outcomes fosters adaptability and perseverance. In contrast, individuals with an external locus of control may struggle to recover from setbacks, as they perceive challenges as insurmountable barriers dictated by external forces.

Cultivating an Internal Locus of Control

Cognitive Restructuring

Cognitive restructuring, a technique used in cognitive-behavioral therapy (CBT), involves identifying and challenging negative thought patterns to develop a more balanced and realistic perspective. By recognizing irrational beliefs and replacing them with empowering thoughts, individuals can shift from an external to an internal locus of control. For example, instead of thinking, "I have no control over my life," one might reframe it to, "I can take steps to influence my circumstances."

Goal Setting and Achievement

Setting and achieving small, manageable goals can help individuals develop a sense of control over their lives. By breaking down larger tasks into achievable steps, individuals can experience success and build confidence in their ability to influence outcomes. This process reinforces an internal locus of control and fosters a proactive mindset.

Mindfulness and Self-Awareness

Practicing mindfulness and developing self-awareness can enhance an internal locus of control by increasing awareness of one's thoughts and behaviors. Mindfulness techniques, such as meditation and journaling, encourage individuals to observe their internal experiences without judgment. This awareness allows for greater control over reactions and fosters a sense of personal agency.

Encouragement and Support

Receiving encouragement and support from others can also help cultivate an internal locus of control. Positive reinforcement from friends, family, or mentors can boost self-esteem and reinforce the belief in one's ability to influence outcomes. Supportive relationships provide a foundation for building resilience and overcoming challenges.

Biblical Insights on Control and Responsibility

Divine Providence and Personal Responsibility

While the Bible acknowledges the role of divine providence, it also emphasizes personal responsibility and the importance of making wise choices. Proverbs 16:9 states, "In their hearts humans plan their course, but the Lord establishes their steps." This verse suggests a balance between trusting in God's plan and taking responsibility for our actions.

Empowerment through Faith

Philippians 4:13 declares, "I can do all things through Christ who strengthens me." This verse underscores the belief in one's ability to overcome challenges with divine support. It aligns with the concept of an internal locus of control, as it encourages believers to take action and trust in their God-given strength and abilities.

Stewardship and Accountability

The parable of the talents in Matthew 25:14-30 illustrates the importance of stewardship and accountability. The servants who wisely invested their talents were rewarded, while the one who buried his talent out of fear was reprimanded. This parable highlights the responsibility to use our abilities and opportunities wisely, reinforcing the principle of personal agency.

Understanding the concept of locus of control and its psychological implications provides valuable insights into how our thoughts influence our circumstances. By cultivating an internal locus of control through cognitive restructuring, goal setting, mindfulness, and supportive relationships, we can enhance our sense of agency and resilience. Integrating biblical principles with psychological insights further enriches our understanding of control and responsibility, empowering us to navigate life's challenges with faith and determination.

Ultimately, the battle between thoughts and circumstances is an ongoing journey that requires intentional effort and self-awareness. By recognizing the power of our perceptions and taking proactive steps to influence our internal and external worlds, we can create a life that reflects our highest values and deepest convictions.

The relationship between our thoughts and the circumstances of our lives is a profound and intricate one, impacting our experiences and shaping our destiny. Psychological theories and philosophical doctrines have long examined this connection, offering various insights into how we can harness the power of our minds to influence our reality. This chapter delves into the psychological concept of locus of control and examines how our perception of control over events can affect our thoughts, emotions, and behaviors. Additionally, we will explore the biblical verse Romans 8:28, which provides a spiritual perspective on the interplay between divine providence and human experience.

The Concept of Locus of Control

Definition and Origins

Locus of control, introduced by psychologist Julian B. Rotter in the 1950s, is a key concept in understanding how individuals perceive the causes of their life experiences and the extent to which they feel in control of these events. It is categorized into two types: internal locus of control and external locus of control.

Internal Locus of Control

Individuals with an internal locus of control believe that they have significant influence over the outcomes in their lives through their actions and decisions. This belief fosters a sense of personal responsibility and empowerment, often leading to higher motivation, resilience, and a proactive approach to challenges.

External Locus of Control

Conversely, those with an external locus of control attribute their experiences to external factors such as luck, fate, or the actions of others. This perspective can lead to feelings of helplessness and a lack of agency, as individuals perceive themselves as being at the mercy of circumstances beyond their control.

Psychological Implications of Locus of Control

Impact on Mental Health

The locus of control plays a crucial role in mental health. An internal locus of control is associated with lower levels of anxiety and depression, as individuals feel more capable of influencing their circumstances and managing stress. On the other hand, an external locus of control is often linked to higher levels of psychological distress, as individuals may feel overwhelmed by forces they believe they cannot control.

Behavioral Outcomes

Locus of control affects behavior across various contexts. Those with an internal locus of control are more likely to engage in goal-setting, persistence, and initiative-taking, viewing themselves as active agents in their lives. In contrast, individuals with an external locus of control may exhibit passivity, avoidance behaviors, and a reluctance to take responsibility for their actions, attributing their outcomes to external factors.

Self-Efficacy and Achievement

Self-efficacy, or the belief in one's ability to succeed in specific situations, is closely linked to locus of control. An internal locus of control enhances self-efficacy, leading to higher achievement and performance across various domains. Conversely, an external locus of control can undermine self-efficacy, resulting in lower motivation and achievement.

Resilience and Adaptability

Resilience, the ability to recover from adversity, is influenced by locus of control. Individuals with an internal locus of control are more likely to view challenges as opportunities for growth, fostering adaptability and perseverance. In contrast, those with an external locus of control may struggle to bounce back from setbacks, perceiving challenges as insurmountable barriers dictated by external forces.

Cultivating an Internal Locus of Control

Cognitive Restructuring

Cognitive restructuring, a technique used in cognitive-behavioral therapy (CBT), involves identifying and challenging negative thought patterns to develop a more balanced and realistic perspective. By recognizing irrational beliefs and replacing them with empowering thoughts, individuals can shift from an external to an internal locus of control. For example, reframing "I have no control over my life" to "I can take steps to influence my circumstances" can significantly alter one's outlook.

Goal Setting and Achievement

Setting and achieving small, manageable goals can help individuals develop a sense of control over their lives. By breaking down larger tasks into achievable steps, individuals can experience success and build confidence in their ability to influence outcomes. This process reinforces an internal locus of control and fosters a proactive mindset.

Mindfulness and Self-Awareness

Practicing mindfulness and developing self-awareness can enhance an internal locus of control by increasing awareness of one's thoughts and behaviors. Mindfulness techniques, such as meditation and journaling, encourage individuals to observe their internal experiences without judgment. This awareness allows for greater control over reactions and fosters a sense of personal agency.

Encouragement and Support

Receiving encouragement and support from others can also help cultivate an internal locus of control. Positive reinforcement from friends, family, or mentors can boost self-esteem and reinforce the belief in one's ability to influence outcomes. Supportive relationships provide a foundation for building resilience and overcoming challenges.

Biblical Insights on Thought and Circumstances

Divine Providence and Personal Responsibility

Romans 8:28 states, "And we know that in all things God works for the good of those who love him." This verse encapsulates the belief in divine providence, suggesting that God orchestrates events for the ultimate good of those who trust in Him. It emphasizes that while we may not always understand the reasons behind our circumstances, we can have faith that they are part of a greater plan for our benefit.

Empowerment through Faith

The Bible teaches that faith in God provides strength and empowerment. Philippians 4:13 declares, "I can do all things through Christ who strengthens me." This verse underscores the belief in one's ability to overcome challenges with divine support. It aligns with the concept of an internal locus of control, as it encourages believers to take action and trust in their God-given strength and abilities.

Stewardship and Accountability

The parable of the talents in Matthew 25:14-30 illustrates the importance of stewardship and accountability. The servants who wisely invested their talents were rewarded, while the one who buried his talent out of fear was reprimanded. This parable highlights the responsibility to use our abilities and opportunities wisely, reinforcing the principle of personal agency.

Hope and Trust in God's Plan

Jeremiah 29:11 offers a message of hope and trust: "For I know the plans I have for you," declares the Lord, "plans to prosper you and not to harm you, plans to give you hope and a future." This verse reassures believers that God's plans are ultimately for their good, even when faced with challenging circumstances. It encourages trust in divine providence while recognizing the role of personal responsibility in aligning with God's purposes.

The interplay between thoughts and circumstances is a complex and multifaceted relationship that has significant implications for our mental health, behavior, and overall well-being. Understanding the concept of locus of control provides valuable insights into how our perceptions of control influence our experiences. By cultivating an internal locus of control through cognitive restructuring, goal setting, mindfulness, and supportive relationships, we can enhance our sense of agency and resilience.

Integrating biblical principles with psychological insights further enriches our understanding of control and responsibility. The Bible's teachings on divine providence, personal empowerment, stewardship, and trust in God's plan offer a balanced perspective on navigating life's challenges. Romans 8:28 serves as a reminder that, even in difficult circumstances, we can trust that God is working for our good.

Ultimately, the journey of aligning our thoughts and circumstances requires intentional effort, self-awareness, and faith. By recognizing the power of our perceptions and taking proactive steps to influence our internal and external worlds, we can create a life that reflects our highest values and deepest convictions, grounded in both psychological wisdom and spiritual faith.

CHAPTER 07

THE EFFECT OF THOUGHT ON HEALTH

The relationship between thought and health is a fundamental aspect of holistic health approaches and the mind-body connection. Philosophical traditions, both ancient and modern, have long recognized that the mind and body are deeply interconnected, and that our mental states can significantly impact our physical well-being. This chapter delves into these philosophical perspectives, examining how our thoughts influence our health and exploring the principles of holistic health.

Holistic Health Approaches

Definition and Principles

Holistic health is an approach that considers the whole person—body, mind, spirit, and emotions—in the quest for optimal health and wellness. According to this philosophy, one can achieve optimal health by gaining proper balance in life. Holistic health practitioners believe that the whole person is made up of interdependent parts, and if one part is not working properly, all the other parts will be affected.

Historical Roots

The concept of holistic health can be traced back to ancient philosophical traditions. For instance, in ancient Greece, Hippocrates, often referred to as the "Father of Medicine," emphasized the importance of balance between the mind and body for overall health. He believed that disease was the result of imbalances in the body and that restoring balance could restore health.

Similarly, in Eastern traditions, such as Traditional Chinese Medicine (TCM) and Ayurveda, the mind-body connection is central to understanding health and disease. TCM, for example, posits that health is achieved by maintaining harmony between the opposing forces of yin and yang and by ensuring the smooth flow of energy (qi) throughout the body. Ayurveda, originating in India, emphasizes the balance of the three doshas (vata, pitta, and kapha) and the alignment of the body, mind, and spirit.

Modern Holistic Health

In contemporary times, holistic health has evolved to incorporate various disciplines, including psychology, nutrition, exercise, and spirituality. Holistic health practitioners use a range of therapies, such as acupuncture, massage, herbal medicine, meditation, and counseling, to promote overall well-being. The emphasis is on preventive care and addressing the root causes of illness rather than merely treating symptoms.

The Mind-Body Connection

Philosophical Perspectives

The mind-body connection refers to the belief that our thoughts, emotions, and attitudes can positively or negatively affect our biological functioning. Philosophers and thinkers across cultures have explored this connection.

René Descartes and Dualism

One of the most influential philosophical perspectives on the mind-body relationship is Cartesian dualism, proposed by René Descartes in the 17th century. Descartes posited that the mind and body are two distinct entities that interact with each other. While his view established a framework for understanding the mind and body as separate, it also laid the groundwork for exploring their interaction.

Spinoza and Monism

In contrast, Baruch Spinoza, a contemporary of Descartes, proposed a monistic view, suggesting that the mind and body are not separate entities but rather two aspects of a single substance. According to Spinoza, mental and physical states are two sides of the same coin, and understanding this unity is crucial for comprehending the nature of existence and well-being.

Holistic Philosophy

Holistic philosophy builds on these ideas, emphasizing that the mind and body are interconnected and interdependent. This perspective suggests that mental and emotional states can influence physical health, and vice versa. For instance, chronic stress, a psychological state, can lead to physical health issues such as hypertension, weakened immune function, and digestive problems.

Thoughts and Physical Health

Psychoneuroimmunology

Psychoneuroimmunology (PNI) is a field of study that investigates the interaction between psychological processes, the nervous system, and the immune system. PNI research has shown that negative thoughts and emotions, such as stress, anxiety, and depression, can weaken the immune system and increase susceptibility to illness. Conversely, positive thoughts and emotions, such as happiness, optimism, and a sense of purpose, can strengthen the immune system and promote better health.

Stress and Health

Stress is one of the most well-documented examples of the mind-body connection. Chronic stress can lead to a range of health problems, including cardiovascular disease, obesity, diabetes, and gastrointestinal disorders. Stress activates the body's "fight-or-flight" response, releasing hormones like cortisol and adrenaline, which, in excess, can have detrimental effects on the body.

Placebo Effect

The placebo effect is another powerful demonstration of the mind-body connection. When patients believe they are receiving treatment, even if it's just a sugar pill, they often experience real improvements in their symptoms. This phenomenon highlights the power of belief and expectation in influencing physical health.

Visualization and Healing

Visualization, or guided imagery, is a technique that involves using the mind to create positive images that can promote healing. Research has shown that visualization can help reduce pain, improve immune function, and enhance overall well-being. Athletes often use visualization to enhance performance, and patients undergoing medical treatments use it to reduce anxiety and improve outcomes.

Integrating Philosophy and Health

Mindfulness and Meditation

Mindfulness and meditation are practices that cultivate a heightened awareness of the present moment and promote relaxation. These practices have roots in both Eastern and Western philosophical traditions and have been shown to reduce stress, lower blood pressure, improve emotional regulation, and enhance overall health.

Stoicism and Resilience

Stoic philosophy, originating in ancient Greece and Rome, teaches the importance of maintaining inner tranquility regardless of external circumstances. Stoics believe that by focusing on what we can control—our thoughts and actions—we can achieve peace of mind and resilience in the face of adversity. This mindset can have profound implications for health, as it promotes a sense of calm and reduces the negative impact of stress.

Positive Thinking and Affirmations

The power of positive thinking is a central tenet in many philosophical and psychological traditions. Affirmations, or positive statements about oneself, can help reframe negative thought patterns and promote a healthier, more optimistic outlook. This shift in mindset can lead to improved physical health by reducing stress and enhancing the body's natural healing processes.

Biblical Insights on Thought and Health

Romans 8:28

Romans 8:28 states, "And we know that in all things God works for the good of those who love him." This verse underscores the belief that God orchestrates events for the ultimate good of believers. It encourages trust in divine providence and suggests that maintaining a positive outlook, rooted in faith, can contribute to overall well-being.

Proverbs 17:22

Proverbs 17:22 highlights the importance of a positive attitude: "A cheerful heart is good medicine, but a crushed spirit dries up the bones." This verse aligns with the holistic health perspective, emphasizing that a positive mindset can promote physical health, while negativity can have detrimental effects.

Philippians 4:8

Philippians 4:8 advises believers to focus on positive thoughts: "Finally, brothers and sisters, whatever is true, whatever is noble, whatever is right, whatever is pure, whatever is lovely, whatever is admirable—if anything is excellent or praiseworthy—think about such things." This exhortation reflects the importance of cultivating positive thoughts to enhance mental and physical well-being.

The effect of thought on health is a profound testament to the interconnectedness of the mind and body. Philosophical traditions, both ancient and modern, recognize that our mental states significantly impact our physical well-being. Holistic health approaches, psychoneuroimmunology, and the mind-body connection all highlight the importance of maintaining a positive, balanced mindset to promote overall health.

By integrating these philosophical insights with biblical principles, we can develop a more comprehensive understanding of how our thoughts influence our health. Trusting in divine providence, cultivating a positive attitude, and focusing on what is noble and praiseworthy can contribute to a healthier, more fulfilling life. As we navigate the complexities of our thoughts and circumstances, embracing a holistic approach can help us achieve optimal health and well-being, grounded in both ancient wisdom and modern understanding.

The relationship between thought and health is a fundamental aspect of understanding overall well-being. Psychological research, particularly in the field of psychoneuroimmunology, has shown how thoughts and emotions can significantly impact physical health. This chapter explores these findings and integrates them with biblical wisdom to provide a comprehensive understanding of how our mental states influence our physical well-being.

Psychoneuroimmunology: Bridging the Mind and Body

Definition and Scope

Psychoneuroimmunology (PNI) is a field of study that explores the interactions between psychological processes, the nervous system, and the immune system. It examines how thoughts, emotions, and behaviors can affect our physical health, particularly through the immune response.

Historical Context

The concept that the mind and body are interconnected has ancient roots. However, PNI emerged as a scientific discipline in the late 20th century, integrating knowledge from psychology, neurology, and immunology. Researchers in this field investigate how stress, emotions, and mental states influence immune function and overall health.

Mechanisms of Influence

PNI research has identified several mechanisms through which thoughts and emotions can impact physical health:

1. Stress Response: Chronic stress activates the body's fight-or-flight response, releasing hormones such as cortisol and adrenaline. While these hormones are essential for immediate survival, prolonged exposure can suppress the immune system, increase inflammation, and contribute to

various health problems, including cardiovascular disease, diabetes, and autoimmune disorders.

2. Neurotransmitters and Hormones: Thoughts and emotions can influence the production and regulation of neurotransmitters and hormones. Positive emotions, such as happiness and love, are associated with the release of endorphins and other "feel-good" chemicals that promote health and well-being. Conversely, negative emotions, such as anxiety and depression, can disrupt hormonal balance and weaken the immune system.

3. Behavioral Pathways: Psychological states can also affect health behaviors. For example, stress and negative emotions may lead to unhealthy coping mechanisms, such as poor diet, lack of exercise, and substance abuse, which can further compromise physical health. Positive mental states, on the other hand, are often associated with healthier lifestyles and better self-care practices.

Impact of Thoughts on Physical Health

Immune System Function

The immune system plays a crucial role in protecting the body against infections, diseases, and foreign invaders. PNI research has shown that mental states can significantly influence immune function:

- Stress and Immunity: Chronic stress can suppress the immune system, making individuals more susceptible to infections and illnesses. Studies have found that stressed individuals have lower levels of natural killer cells, which are essential for combating viruses and cancer cells.

- Positive Emotions and Immunity: Positive emotions and a sense of well-being can enhance immune function. Research has shown that individuals with positive mental states have higher levels of antibodies and other immune markers, indicating a stronger immune response.

Cardiovascular Health

Thoughts and emotions also have a profound impact on cardiovascular health:

- Stress and Heart Disease: Chronic stress and negative emotions, such as anger and hostility, are associated with an increased risk of heart disease. Stress can raise blood pressure, increase heart rate, and contribute to the buildup of arterial plaque.

- Positive Mental States and Heart Health: Positive emotions, such as joy, gratitude, and love, can protect against heart disease by lowering blood pressure, reducing inflammation, and improving overall cardiovascular function.

Digestive Health

The digestive system is highly sensitive to emotional and psychological states:

- Stress and Digestive Disorders: Stress and negative emotions can exacerbate digestive disorders, such as irritable bowel syndrome (IBS) and inflammatory bowel disease (IBD). Stress can alter gut motility, increase stomach acid production, and disrupt the balance of gut microbiota.

- Positive Emotions and Digestion: Positive mental states can promote healthy digestion by regulating gut motility, enhancing nutrient absorption, and maintaining a balanced gut microbiome.

Biblical Insights on Thought and Health

Proverbs 17:22

The Bible provides profound insights into the connection between thoughts and health. Proverbs 17:22 states, "A cheerful heart is good medicine, but a crushed spirit dries up the bones." This verse highlights the importance of maintaining a positive attitude for physical well-being. A cheerful heart, filled with joy and gratitude, can act as a natural medicine, promoting health and healing. In contrast, a crushed spirit, burdened by negative thoughts and emotions, can have detrimental effects on the body.

The Healing Power of Joy

Joy and positive emotions are emphasized throughout the Bible as essential for a healthy and fulfilling life. For instance, Nehemiah 8:10 says, "The joy of the Lord is your strength." This verse suggests that joy derived from a relationship with God can provide strength and resilience, both mentally and physically. Embracing joy can lead to a more robust immune system, better cardiovascular health, and overall well-being.

Managing Negative Emotions

The Bible also addresses the impact of negative emotions on health. For example, Psalm 42:11 states, "Why, my soul, are you downcast? Why so disturbed within me? Put your hope in God, for I will yet praise him, my Savior and my God." This verse encourages individuals to manage negative emotions by turning to God and maintaining hope and faith. By doing so, one can alleviate the burden of negative thoughts and promote mental and physical health.

Integrating Psychology and Biblical Wisdom

Cognitive Behavioral Therapy (CBT)

Cognitive Behavioral Therapy (CBT) is a psychological approach that aligns well with biblical principles. CBT focuses on identifying and changing negative thought patterns to improve emotional and physical well-being. By replacing negative thoughts with positive, realistic ones, individuals can reduce stress, improve immune function, and enhance overall health. This approach is similar to the biblical exhortation to "renew your mind" (Romans 12:2) and focus on positive, uplifting thoughts (Philippians 4:8).

Mindfulness and Prayer

Mindfulness practices, which involve focusing on the present moment and cultivating a non-judgmental awareness, can also promote health and well-being. When combined with prayer, mindfulness can help individuals manage stress, reduce anxiety, and improve mental and physical health. The Bible encourages mindfulness in the form of prayer and meditation, as seen in Psalm 46:10: "Be still, and know that I am God."

Gratitude and Well-Being

Gratitude is another powerful tool for enhancing health. Studies have shown that practicing gratitude can improve mental health, boost immune function, and increase overall well-being. The Bible frequently emphasizes the importance of gratitude, as in 1 Thessalonians 5:18: "Give thanks in all circumstances; for this is God's will for you in Christ Jesus." By cultivating gratitude, individuals can foster a positive mindset and promote better health.

The effect of thought on health is a testament to the profound connection between the mind and body. Psychoneuroimmunology provides a scientific framework for understanding how our mental states influence our physical well-being, while biblical wisdom offers timeless insights into the importance of maintaining a positive, joyful attitude.

By integrating these perspectives, we can develop a more holistic approach to health. Embracing joy, managing negative emotions, and cultivating gratitude can lead to a healthier, more fulfilling life. As Proverbs 17:22 reminds us, "A cheerful heart is good medicine," highlighting the power of positive thoughts to promote healing and well-being. By nurturing our mental and emotional health, we can enhance our physical health and achieve a balanced, harmonious life.

CHAPTER 08

THOUGHT AND PURPOSE

The search for purpose is a central theme in human existence, influencing our thoughts, actions, and overall well-being. Philosophers throughout history have explored this quest for meaning, emphasizing its importance in shaping our lives. This chapter delves into the philosophical perspectives of Viktor Frankl and Friedrich Nietzsche, examining their views on purpose and how our thoughts play a crucial role in discovering and fulfilling them.

Viktor Frankl: Meaning and the Will to Purpose

Existential Philosophy and Logotherapy

Viktor Frankl, an Austrian neurologist, psychiatrist, and Holocaust survivor, developed logotherapy, a form of existential analysis that emphasizes the search for meaning as the primary motivation in human life. Frankl's experiences in

Nazi concentration camps profoundly shaped his understanding of purpose and the human spirit's resilience.

The Search for Meaning

In his seminal work, "Man's Search for Meaning," Frankl argues that life has meaning under all circumstances, even the most miserable ones. He posits that our primary drive is not pleasure (as Freud suggested) or power (as Adler believed) but the pursuit of what we find meaningful. Frankl's philosophy is rooted in the idea that finding purpose can help individuals endure suffering and overcome existential crises.

Three Paths to Meaning

Frankl outlines three ways to discover meaning in life:

1. Through Work: Engaging in meaningful work and creative activities can provide a sense of purpose. This aligns with the idea that our thoughts and efforts should be directed towards productive and fulfilling endeavors.

2. Through Love: Building deep, loving relationships allows us to find meaning in connection with others. Frankl emphasizes that love enriches our existence and helps us transcend our individual limitations.

3. Through Suffering: Even in unavoidable suffering, we can find purpose by adopting a meaningful attitude towards it. Frankl asserts that suffering if faced with courage

and dignity, can lead to personal growth and a deeper understanding of life.

Frankl's Impact on Modern Thought

Frankl's emphasis on the importance of purpose has had a lasting impact on psychology and philosophy. His work highlights the transformative power of thoughts focused on meaning and purpose, suggesting that a purposeful mindset can help individuals navigate life's challenges and find fulfillment.

Friedrich Nietzsche: The Will to Power and Purpose

Nietzsche's Existentialism

Friedrich Nietzsche, a German philosopher known for his provocative ideas and critiques of traditional values, explored the concept of purpose through his philosophy of the "will to power." Nietzsche's existentialist approach emphasizes individualism, self-overcoming, and the creation of personal meaning.

The Will to Power

Nietzsche posited that the fundamental driving force in humans is the "will to power," the desire to assert and enhance one's existence. This concept extends beyond the pursuit of dominance and control, encompassing the drive for self-improvement, creativity, and the realization of one's potential.

Purpose and Self-Overcoming

Nietzsche believed that finding purpose involves a process of self-overcoming, where individuals strive to transcend their limitations and create their own values. He rejected the idea of preordained purpose, instead advocating for a self-determined approach to meaning:

1. Creating Personal Values: Nietzsche argued that individuals must create their own values and purpose, rather than relying on external sources or societal norms. This involves critical self-reflection and the courage to challenge conventional beliefs.

2. The Übermensch (Overman): Nietzsche introduced the concept of the Übermensch, an idealized individual who has overcome the constraints of ordinary existence and achieved a higher state of being. The Übermensch embodies the ultimate realization of purpose through self-mastery and the creation of meaning.

3. Embracing the Eternal Recurrence: Nietzsche's idea of the eternal recurrence, the notion that life endlessly repeats itself, serves as a test of one's commitment to their chosen purpose. He challenged individuals to live in a way that they would gladly repeat for eternity, thus emphasizing the importance of living purposefully and authentically.

Nietzsche's Legacy

Nietzsche's existentialist philosophy has influenced various fields, from psychology to literature. His emphasis on self-determined purpose and the will to power resonates with contemporary ideas about personal growth and the importance of a purposeful mindset.

Integrating Thought and Purpose

The Power of Purposeful Thinking

Both Frankl and Nietzsche highlight the crucial role of thoughts in finding and fulfilling purpose. Purposeful thinking involves focusing our mental energy on meaningful goals, values, and aspirations. By aligning our thoughts with our purpose, we can:

1. Enhance Motivation: Purposeful thinking fuels motivation and drive, helping us to overcome obstacles and stay committed to our goals.

2. Cultivate Resilience: A strong sense of purpose can provide the mental strength needed to endure challenges and setbacks, fostering resilience and perseverance.

3. Promote Well-Being: Research has shown that individuals with a clear sense of purpose experience greater life satisfaction, better mental health, and improved physical health. Purposeful thoughts contribute to a more fulfilling and balanced life.

Practical Steps to Cultivate Purposeful Thinking

1. Reflect on Values and Passions: Take time to identify your core values and passions. What matters most to you? What activities or causes ignite your enthusiasm? Reflecting on these questions can help you clarify your purpose.

2. Set Meaningful Goals: Establish goals that align with your values and passions. Ensure that these goals are specific, measurable, and attainable, providing a clear direction for your thoughts and actions.

3. Practice Mindfulness: Mindfulness practices, such as meditation and journaling, can help you stay focused on your purpose. Regularly revisiting your goals and reflecting on your progress can reinforce purposeful thinking.

4. Surround Yourself with Support: Build a supportive network of friends, mentors, and like-minded individuals who share your values and aspirations. Their encouragement and insights can help you stay aligned with your purpose.

5. Embrace Challenges: View challenges as opportunities for growth and self-overcoming. Embrace the process of striving towards your purpose, even when faced with difficulties.

Biblical Insights on Thought and Purpose

Jeremiah 29:11

The Bible provides valuable insights into the concept of purpose. Jeremiah 29:11 states, "For I know the plans I have for you, declares the Lord, plans for welfare and not for evil, to give you a future and a hope." This verse emphasizes that God has a purpose and plan for each individual, offering hope and guidance in the search for meaning.

Purpose in Work and Service

The Bible also highlights the importance of work and service in discovering and fulfilling purpose. Colossians 3:23-24 encourages believers to "work heartily, as for the Lord and not for men, knowing that from the Lord you will receive the inheritance as your reward." This passage suggests that purposeful work, done with dedication and integrity, can lead to a sense of fulfillment and divine reward.

Purpose in Suffering

Similar to Frankl's perspective, the Bible acknowledges that purpose can be found even in suffering. Romans 5:3-4 states, "Not only that, but we rejoice in our sufferings, knowing that suffering produces endurance, and endurance produces character, and character produces hope." This verse underscores the idea that enduring suffering with a meaningful attitude can lead to personal growth and deeper purpose.

The exploration of thought and purpose through the philosophies of Viktor Frankl and Friedrich Nietzsche reveals the profound impact of our mental states on our quest for meaning. Frankl's emphasis on the search for meaning and Nietzsche's advocacy for self-determined purpose both highlight the transformative power of purposeful thinking.

Integrating these philosophical insights with biblical wisdom provides a comprehensive understanding of how purpose shapes our lives. By cultivating purposeful thoughts, reflecting on our values, and embracing challenges, we can discover and fulfill our unique purpose, leading to a more meaningful and fulfilling existence. As we navigate life's journey, let us remember the words of Jeremiah 29:11, trusting in the divine plan and embracing the hope and future that purpose brings.

Purpose is a driving force in human life, guiding our actions, decisions, and overall sense of fulfillment. In this chapter, we explore the psychological framework of goal-setting theory and its connection to the importance of having a purpose. We will also reflect on the biblical wisdom found in Jeremiah 29:11, which emphasizes the divine plan for our lives. Together, these perspectives illuminate the power of thought in shaping our purpose and directing our lives.

Goal-Setting Theory and the Psychology of Purpose

Understanding Goal-Setting Theory

Goal-setting theory, developed by psychologists Edwin Locke and Gary Latham, emphasizes the critical role of setting specific, challenging goals in enhancing motivation, performance, and personal satisfaction. According to this theory, having clear goals directs attention, mobilizes effort, increases persistence, and encourages the development of strategies to achieve objectives.

Key Components of Goal-Setting Theory

1. Clarity: Clear, specific goals provide a precise direction for our efforts, reducing ambiguity and enhancing focus. When goals are well-defined, individuals can more easily measure their progress and stay motivated.

2. Challenge: Goals should be challenging yet attainable. Difficult goals push individuals to stretch their abilities and achieve higher levels of performance, fostering personal growth and development.

3. Commitment: Commitment to a goal is crucial for its successful attainment. Individuals must be genuinely dedicated to their goals, believe in their importance, and be willing to invest the necessary effort.

4. Feedback: Regular feedback is essential for monitoring progress and making necessary adjustments.

Feedback helps individuals stay on track, recognize achievements, and identify areas for improvement.

5. Task Complexity: The complexity of a task should match an individual's capabilities. While challenging goals are beneficial, overly complex tasks can lead to frustration and decreased motivation. It is important to break down complex goals into manageable steps.

The Role of Purpose in Goal-Setting

Purpose provides the overarching framework within which specific goals are set. It is the why behind our actions, the reason we strive towards certain objectives. Having a clear sense of purpose enhances the effectiveness of goal-setting by:

1. Providing Meaning: Purpose imbues goals with significance, making them more meaningful and motivating. When individuals understand how their goals align with their broader purpose, they are more likely to stay committed and persevere through challenges.

2. Guiding Decision-Making: Purpose acts as a compass, guiding decisions and helping individuals prioritize their goals. It provides a sense of direction, ensuring that the goals set are in harmony with one's values and long-term aspirations.

3. Enhancing Resilience: A strong sense of purpose can buffer against setbacks and failures. When individuals are driven by a deep sense of purpose, they are more likely to view obstacles as temporary and remain resilient in the face of adversity.

The Importance of Having a Purpose

Purpose and Well-Being

Research has consistently shown that having a clear sense of purpose is associated with numerous psychological benefits, including increased life satisfaction, improved mental health, and greater overall well-being. Purpose provides a sense of coherence and direction, contributing to a more fulfilling and meaningful life.

1. Life Satisfaction: Individuals with a strong sense of purpose report higher levels of life satisfaction. Purposeful living involves engaging in activities that are meaningful and aligned with one's values, leading to a greater sense of contentment.

2. Mental Health: Purpose is linked to better mental health outcomes, including lower levels of depression and anxiety. A sense of purpose provides individuals with a reason to persevere, fostering hope and resilience.

3. Physical Health: Purposeful individuals also tend to have better physical health. Research suggests that having a

sense of purpose can reduce the risk of chronic diseases, improve immune function, and promote longevity.

Purpose Across the Lifespan

Purpose is relevant at all stages of life, influencing how individuals navigate various life transitions and challenges.

1. Adolescence: During adolescence, the search for purpose is a critical developmental task. Young people explore their identities, values, and aspirations, laying the foundation for a purposeful adulthood.

2. Adulthood: In adulthood, purpose often centers around career, family, and personal goals. Having a clear sense of purpose can enhance job satisfaction, improve relationships, and provide a sense of fulfillment.

3. Later Life: In later life, maintaining a sense of purpose is vital for psychological well-being and life satisfaction. Older adults may find purpose through mentoring, volunteering, or pursuing passions that contribute to a sense of legacy and meaning.

Integrating Biblical Wisdom on Purpose

Jeremiah 29:11

Jeremiah 29:11 states, "For I know the plans I have for you, declares the Lord, plans for welfare and not for evil, to give you a future and a hope." This verse underscores the belief that God has a purpose and plan for each individual's life, offering hope and assurance in the search for meaning.

Divine Purpose and Human Agency

The Bible teaches that while God has a plan for each person, individuals also have the agency to pursue their purpose actively. Proverbs 16:9 states, "The heart of man plans his way, but the Lord establishes his steps." This suggests a partnership between human effort and divine guidance, where individuals are encouraged to set goals and work towards them, trusting in God's overarching plan.

Purpose in Service

The Bible emphasizes the importance of serving others as a means of fulfilling one's purpose. Galatians 5:13 encourages believers to "serve one another humbly in love." Serving others not only benefits the community but also provides a deep sense of purpose and fulfillment.

Overcoming Obstacles with Purpose

Romans 8:28 reassures believers that "in all things, God works for the good of those who love him, who have been called according to his purpose." This verse highlights that even in the face of challenges and setbacks, a strong sense of purpose can provide hope and resilience, knowing that God's plan is ultimately for good.

Practical Steps to Cultivate Purpose

1. Reflect on Your Values: Identify your core values and beliefs. What principles guide your decisions and actions? Reflecting on your values can help clarify your purpose and align your goals with what matters most to you.

2. Set Meaningful Goals: Establish goals that are aligned with your values and long-term aspirations. Ensure that your goals are specific, measurable, attainable, relevant, and time-bound (SMART).

3. Seek Feedback and Reflection: Regularly seek feedback and reflect on your progress. This can help you stay on track, make necessary adjustments, and reinforce your commitment to your purpose.

4. Engage in Service: Find opportunities to serve others in ways that align with your purpose. Serving others can provide a deep sense of fulfillment and reinforce your sense of purpose.

5. Trust in Divine Guidance: Trust in the divine plan for your life, as emphasized in Jeremiah 29:11. Seek guidance through prayer, meditation, and reflection, and remain open to the ways in which your purpose may unfold.

The integration of goal-setting theory, the psychological benefits of purpose, and biblical wisdom provide a comprehensive understanding of the importance of having a purpose. Purposeful thinking and living are crucial for personal growth, resilience, and overall well-being. By aligning our thoughts with meaningful goals and trusting in the divine plan, we can navigate life's journey with a clear sense of direction and fulfillment. Let us embrace the promise of Jeremiah 29:11, knowing that our lives are part of a greater purpose and plan.

CHAPTER 09

THE THOUGHT FACTOR IN ACHIEVEMENT

Achievement is often seen as the pinnacle of personal and professional success. While hard work, talent, and opportunity play significant roles, the power of thought is a crucial, yet sometimes overlooked, component in achieving excellence. This chapter delves into the philosophical perspectives of Confucius and Aristotle on the role of thought in achievement, providing insights into how our mental attitudes and thought processes can drive us toward excellence.

Confucius on Thought and Achievement

The Importance of Self-Cultivation

Confucius, one of the most influential philosophers in Eastern philosophy, emphasized the importance of self-cultivation and the development of one's character as the foundation for achievement. According to Confucius, personal excellence is achieved through continuous self-improvement and the cultivation of virtues such as benevolence, righteousness, propriety, wisdom, and faithfulness.

1. Reflection and Learning: Confucius believed that reflection and learning are key to personal growth and achievement. He famously stated, "By three methods we may learn wisdom: First, by reflection, which is noblest; Second, by imitation, which is easiest; and third by experience, which is the bitterest." Reflective thought allows individuals to learn from their experiences and make informed decisions that lead to success.

2. Moral Integrity: For Confucius, moral integrity is a prerequisite for true achievement. He taught that one must cultivate their inner virtues to achieve external success. "The superior man is modest in his speech, but exceeds in his actions," he asserted, highlighting the importance of aligning one's thoughts and actions with moral principles.

3. Role of Thought in Governance: Confucius also emphasized the role of thought in governance and leadership. He believed that a ruler's thoughts and moral character directly influence the well-being of the state. "The superior man understands what is right; the inferior man understands what will sell," he observed, suggesting that thought guided by virtue leads to genuine achievement and prosperity.

Aristotle on Thought and Achievement

The Pursuit of Excellence

Aristotle, a towering figure in Western philosophy, offered profound insights into the nature of thought and achievement. He introduced the concept of "eudaimonia," often translated as "flourishing" or "well-being," which is achieved through the pursuit of virtue and excellence.

1. The Role of Rational Thought: Aristotle emphasized the role of rational thought in achieving excellence. He believed that humans are rational beings, and the highest form of achievement is realized through the exercise of reason. "Excellence is never an accident. It is always the result of high intention, sincere effort, and intelligent execution; it represents the wise choice of many alternatives," he stated, underscoring the importance of deliberate and rational thought in the pursuit of excellence.

2. Virtue and Habit: For Aristotle, virtue is achieved through the cultivation of good habits. He argued that virtuous actions arise from a well-ordered soul, where rational thought guides desires and emotions. "We are what we repeatedly do. Excellence, then, is not an act, but a habit," he proclaimed, highlighting the role of consistent, thoughtful actions in achieving excellence.

3. The Golden Mean: Aristotle's concept of the "Golden Mean" emphasizes the importance of balance and moderation in thought and action. He believed that virtue lies between excess and deficiency, and rational thought is essential in finding this balance. "Moral virtue is a mean between two vices, one of excess and the other of deficiency," he asserted, suggesting that thoughtful moderation leads to enduring achievement.

Integrating Philosophical Insights into Modern Achievement

Practical Applications

1. Cultivating Virtue: Drawing from Confucius and Aristotle, cultivating personal virtues is essential for achieving excellence. Reflect on your values and strive to develop qualities such as integrity, wisdom, and resilience. Align your thoughts and actions with these virtues to build a strong foundation for success.

2. Continuous Learning and Reflection: Embrace a mindset of continuous learning and reflection. Regularly evaluate your experiences, learn from them, and apply these lessons to future endeavors. This practice enhances your ability to make informed decisions and achieve your goals.

3. Rational Decision-Making: Develop your rational thinking skills to make intelligent and informed decisions.

Weigh the pros and cons of various options, consider long-term consequences, and choose actions that align with your values and objectives.

4. Building Good Habits: Focus on building and maintaining good habits. Consistent, thoughtful actions lead to lasting excellence. Identify key habits that contribute to your goals and practice them regularly.

5. Balancing Extremes: Strive for balance in your thoughts and actions. Avoid extremes and seek the Golden Mean, where virtue and excellence reside. This balanced approach leads to sustainable achievement and well-being.

Biblical Perspective on Thought and Achievement

"Do not be conformed to this world, but be transformed by the renewal of your mind." (Romans 12:2)

The Bible also underscores the importance of thought in achieving excellence. Romans 12:2 encourages believers to renew their minds, suggesting that transformative thinking leads to genuine achievement. This verse aligns with the philosophical insights of Confucius and Aristotle, emphasizing the power of thoughtful reflection and rational decision-making.

Renewing the Mind for Achievement

1. Spiritual Growth: Renewing the mind involves spiritual growth and aligning one's thoughts with divine

principles. Engage in practices such as prayer, meditation, and studying scripture to cultivate a mindset that honors God and promotes personal excellence.

2. Positive Thinking: Embrace positive thinking and reject negative, self-limiting thoughts. Philippians 4:8 advises believers to think about things that are true, noble, right, pure, lovely, and admirable. Positive thoughts lead to positive actions and outcomes.

3. Trust in God's Plan: Trusting in God's plan for your life is essential for achieving true excellence. Jeremiah 29:11 reassures believers that God has plans for their welfare and success. Align your thoughts with God's promises and trust in His guidance as you pursue your goals.

4. Perseverance and Faith: Achieving excellence often requires perseverance and faith. Hebrews 12:1 encourages believers to "run with perseverance the race marked out for us." Maintain a steadfast mindset, and trust that God will provide the strength and wisdom needed to achieve your goals.

The integration of Confucian and Aristotelian philosophy, along with biblical wisdom, provides a comprehensive understanding of the role of thought in achieving excellence. By cultivating virtues, engaging in continuous learning, practicing rational decision-making, and renewing our minds, we can harness the power of thought to achieve our highest potential. Let us embrace the transformative power of thought, guided by wisdom and faith, to achieve excellence in all aspects of life.

Achievement, whether personal or professional, is often seen as the culmination of hard work, talent, and opportunity. However, an equally important yet sometimes overlooked component is the power of thought. This chapter examines the role of thought in achieving excellence from psychological and biblical perspectives, providing insights into how our mental attitudes and processes can drive us toward success.

The Psychology of Success

The Growth Mindset

One of the most influential concepts in the psychology of success is the growth mindset, introduced by psychologist Carol Dweck. The growth mindset is the belief that abilities and intelligence can be developed through dedication, hard work, and learning. This stands in contrast to a fixed mindset, where individuals believe their talents and abilities are static and unchangeable.

1. Embracing Challenges: People with a growth mindset see challenges as opportunities to grow rather than obstacles to avoid. This perspective encourages persistence

and resilience. When faced with a difficult task, those with a growth mindset are more likely to persevere and find creative solutions.

2. Learning from Criticism: Feedback and criticism are viewed as valuable sources of information in a growth mindset. Instead of taking criticism personally, individuals use it to improve their skills and performance. This open attitude toward feedback fosters continuous improvement and learning.

3. The Power of Effort: Effort is seen as a pathway to mastery in a growth mindset. Individuals understand that hard work and perseverance are essential components of success. This contrasts with the fixed mindset, where effort might be seen as a sign of inadequacy.

4. Celebrating Others' Success: People with a growth mindset find inspiration in others' successes rather than feeling threatened. They believe that there is enough success to go around and that learning from others' achievements can provide valuable insights for their own growth.

Self-Efficacy and Achievement

Self-efficacy, a concept introduced by psychologist Albert Bandura, refers to an individual's belief in their ability to succeed in specific situations. High self-efficacy can enhance motivation and performance by fostering a sense of control over one's actions and outcomes.

1. Setting Realistic Goals: High self-efficacy encourages individuals to set challenging but attainable goals. They believe in their capacity to achieve these goals, which enhances their motivation and commitment.

2. Persistence in the Face of Adversity: Individuals with high self-efficacy are more likely to persist in the face of obstacles. They view setbacks as temporary and surmountable, rather than as indications of personal failure.

3. Influence on Emotional States: High self-efficacy can positively influence emotional states. Individuals with strong self-efficacy are less likely to experience anxiety and more likely to approach tasks with enthusiasm and confidence.

4. Impact on Learning and Performance: Belief in one's ability to learn and perform well can lead to greater effort and perseverance. This can result in improved performance and the acquisition of new skills, creating a positive feedback loop that further enhances self-efficacy.

Biblical Perspective on Thought and Achievement

"Commit to the Lord whatever you do, and he will establish your plans." (Proverbs 16:3)

The Bible offers profound insights into the role of thought and commitment in achieving success. Proverbs 16:3 emphasizes the importance of dedicating our efforts to the Lord, suggesting that when we align our plans with divine will, we are more likely to achieve our goals.

Aligning Thoughts with Divine Purpose

1. Commitment to God: Committing our plans to the Lord involves aligning our thoughts and actions with His will. This requires regular prayer, reflection, and seeking guidance from scripture. By dedicating our efforts to God, we invite His wisdom and strength into our pursuits.

2. Trust in God's Guidance: Trusting in God's guidance provides a sense of peace and confidence. Philippians 4:13 states, "I can do all things through Christ who strengthens me." This verse reminds believers that divine support is available, empowering them to overcome challenges and achieve their goals.

3. Faith and Action: James 2:17 teaches that "faith by itself, if it is not accompanied by action, is dead." This highlights the importance of combining faith with diligent effort. Believers are encouraged to take proactive steps toward their goals, trusting that God will bless their efforts.

4. Perseverance and Patience: Hebrews 12:1 encourages believers to "run with perseverance the race

marked out for us." This scripture underscores the importance of enduring faith and patience in the pursuit of long-term goals. By maintaining a steadfast mindset, believers can overcome obstacles and achieve lasting success.

The Power of Positive Thinking

1. Meditating on Positive Thoughts: Philippians 4:8 advises believers to think about things that are true, noble, right, pure, lovely, and admirable. Positive thinking can transform one's attitude and approach to challenges, leading to more favorable outcomes.

2. Renewing the Mind: Romans 12:2 encourages believers to "be transformed by the renewal of your mind." This involves replacing negative, self-limiting thoughts with positive, faith-filled ones. Renewing the mind can lead to a more optimistic outlook and greater resilience in the face of adversity.

3. Gratitude and Contentment: 1 Thessalonians 5:18 urges believers to "give thanks in all circumstances." Practicing gratitude can shift one's focus from what is lacking to what is abundant, fostering a sense of contentment and joy. This positive mindset can enhance overall well-being and achievement.

Integrating Psychological and Biblical Insights
Practical Applications

1. Developing a Growth Mindset: Embrace challenges, learn from criticism, and view effort as a path to mastery. Combine this with a commitment to God, seeking His guidance and strength in all endeavors.

2. Enhancing Self-Efficacy: Set realistic goals, persist in the face of adversity, and maintain a positive emotional state. Trust in God's plan and believe in your ability to succeed through His strength.

3. Practicing Positive Thinking: Focus on positive, faith-filled thoughts and meditate on scripture. Regularly renew your mind and practice gratitude to cultivate a positive and resilient mindset.

4. Combining Faith with Action: Take proactive steps toward your goals, combining diligent effort with steadfast faith. Trust that God will bless your efforts and provide the necessary guidance and support.

The integration of psychological principles, such as the growth mindset and self-efficacy, with biblical wisdom provides a comprehensive understanding of the role of thought in achieving excellence. By cultivating a growth mindset, enhancing self-efficacy, practicing positive thinking, and committing our efforts to God, we can harness the transformative power of thought to achieve our highest potential. Let us embrace the thought-factor in achievement, guided by psychological insights and biblical wisdom, to realize success in all aspects of life.

179

CHAPTER 10

VISIONS AND IDEALS

Visions and ideals serve as the guiding stars in our personal development journey. They give us direction, purpose, and motivation. By setting high standards and envisioning our best selves, we create a framework for growth and achievement. This chapter delves into the philosophical importance of vision and ideals, their psychological impact, and the biblical wisdom that supports their significance in personal development.

The Philosophical Perspective

The Role of Vision

1. Socrates and the Unexamined Life: Socrates famously stated, "The unexamined life is not worth living." This assertion underscores the importance of self-reflection and the pursuit of personal ideals. A vision for one's life

requires regular introspection and a commitment to personal growth.

2. Plato's Theory of Forms: Plato's philosophy introduces the concept of the Forms, idealized versions of everything in the physical world. This notion suggests that our visions and ideals represent the highest potential we can strive for. By aspiring to these ideals, we align ourselves with the pursuit of truth, beauty, and goodness.

3. Aristotle and Eudaimonia: Aristotle's concept of eudaimonia, often translated as "flourishing" or "the good life," is achieved by living in accordance with reason and virtue. He argued that having a clear vision of one's highest potential and striving to embody virtues such as courage, wisdom, and justice leads to true fulfillment.

The Importance of Ideals

1. Confucian Virtue Ethics: Confucius emphasized the cultivation of virtues and the importance of moral ideals. He believed that by striving toward ideals such as ren (benevolence), yi (righteousness), and li (propriety), individuals could achieve personal and social harmony.

2. Nietzsche's Übermensch: Friedrich Nietzsche introduced the concept of the Übermensch, or "superman," as an ideal for humanity to strive towards. This vision represents a future individual who has transcended

conventional morals and societal limitations to create their own values and meaning.

3. Viktor Frankl's Logotherapy: Viktor Frankl, a Holocaust survivor and psychiatrist, developed logotherapy based on the idea that the search for meaning is a primary motivational force. He argued that having a vision or ideal gives individuals a sense of purpose and helps them endure and overcome life's challenges.

Psychological Insights

The Power of Visualization

1. Mental Imagery and Performance: Research in psychology has shown that visualization, or mental imagery, can significantly enhance performance in various domains, including sports, academics, and professional pursuits. Athletes, for instance, often use visualization techniques to improve their skills and achieve their goals.

2. Creating a Mental Blueprint: Visualization involves creating a detailed mental image of a desired outcome. This mental blueprint helps individuals focus their efforts, maintain motivation, and build confidence. By repeatedly envisioning success, individuals can reinforce positive beliefs and behaviors that contribute to their goals.

Setting and Pursuing Ideals

1. Goal-Setting Theory: Edwin Locke and Gary Latham's goal-setting theory emphasizes the importance of setting specific, challenging goals to enhance performance. Clear visions and ideals provide a sense of direction and purpose, making it easier to develop actionable steps toward achieving them.

2. Intrinsic and Extrinsic Motivation: Ideals often tap into intrinsic motivation, which is driven by internal satisfaction and personal fulfillment. Pursuing a vision or ideal that aligns with one's values and passions can lead to greater persistence, creativity, and overall well-being.

3. Self-Actualization: According to Abraham Maslow's hierarchy of needs, self-actualization represents the fulfillment of one's potential and the realization of personal ideals. This highest level of psychological development involves the pursuit of meaningful goals, personal growth, and the expression of one's true self.

Biblical Wisdom

"Where there is no vision, the people perish." (Proverbs 29:18)

The Bible underscores the importance of having a vision and ideals to guide our lives. Proverbs 29:18 highlights that without a vision, people lose their way and fail to reach their full potential. This verse emphasizes the necessity of having a clear sense of purpose and direction.

Biblical Examples of Vision and Ideals

1. Joseph's Dreams: In the book of Genesis, Joseph's dreams of greatness gave him a vision for his future, even when faced with adversity. His unwavering faith in his God-given vision ultimately led to his rise to power and the fulfillment of his dreams (Genesis 37-41).

2. Nehemiah's Vision for Jerusalem: Nehemiah had a vision to rebuild the walls of Jerusalem, driven by his commitment to God and his people. Despite opposition and challenges, his clear vision and dedication led to the successful completion of the project (Nehemiah 1-6).

3. Paul's Mission: The Apostle Paul had a vision of spreading the gospel to the Gentiles. His unwavering commitment to this divine mission, despite numerous trials and persecutions, resulted in the establishment of many early Christian communities (Acts 9, 13-28).

The Role of Faith and Hope

1. Faith as Assurance: Hebrews 11:1 defines faith as "the assurance of things hoped for, the conviction of things not seen." Having a vision and ideals requires faith in their eventual realization, even when they are not immediately visible.

2. Hope as an Anchor: Hebrews 6:19 describes hope as "an anchor for the soul, firm and secure." A vision or ideal provides hope, anchoring individuals in difficult times and giving them the strength to persevere.

3. Transforming Vision into Reality: Ephesians 3:20 states, "Now to him who is able to do immeasurably more than all we ask or imagine, according to his power that is at work within us." This verse encourages believers to trust in God's ability to bring their visions and ideals to fruition.

Integrating Philosophical, Psychological, and Biblical Insights

Practical Applications

1. Define Your Vision: Reflect on your deepest values, passions, and aspirations. Create a clear and compelling vision that aligns with your beliefs and desires.

2. Visualize Success: Regularly practice visualization techniques to create a mental image of your desired outcomes. Use these images to motivate and guide your actions.

3. Set Clear Goals: Break down your vision into specific, achievable goals. Develop a step-by-step plan to reach these goals, and regularly review and adjust your progress.

4. Cultivate a Growth Mindset: Embrace challenges, learn from setbacks, and view effort as essential to achieving

your ideals. Maintain a positive attitude and a willingness to grow.

5. Seek Divine Guidance: Commit your vision and goals to God, seeking His wisdom and strength. Trust in His plans and remain open to His guidance throughout your journey.

Visions and ideals are powerful forces that shape our lives, providing direction, purpose, and motivation. By integrating philosophical insights, psychological principles, and biblical wisdom, we can harness the creative power of thought to achieve our highest potential. Let us strive to define and pursue our visions and ideals, guided by faith and a commitment to personal growth, to lead fulfilling and impactful lives.

Visions and ideals act as the guiding stars in our journey of personal development. They provide direction, purpose, and motivation, shaping the paths we take and the goals we pursue. This chapter explores the philosophical importance of visions and ideals, their psychological impact on motivation and self-actualization, and the biblical wisdom that underscores their significance in our lives.

Philosophical Perspectives

The Role of Vision in Personal Development

1. Socrates and the Unexamined Life: Socrates famously declared, "The unexamined life is not worth living." This statement underscores the importance of self-reflection and the pursuit of personal ideals. A vision for one's life requires regular introspection and a commitment to personal growth.

2. Plato's Theory of Forms: Plato's philosophy introduces the concept of the Forms, idealized versions of everything in the physical world. This notion suggests that our visions and ideals represent the highest potential we can strive for. By aspiring to these ideals, we align ourselves with the pursuit of truth, beauty, and goodness.

3. Aristotle and Eudaimonia: Aristotle's concept of eudaimonia, often translated as "flourishing" or "the good life," is achieved by living in accordance with reason and virtue. He argued that having a clear vision of one's highest potential and striving to embody virtues such as courage, wisdom, and justice leads to true fulfillment.

The Importance of Ideals

1. Confucian Virtue Ethics: Confucius emphasized the cultivation of virtues and the importance of moral ideals. He believed that by striving toward ideals such as ren (benevolence), yi (righteousness), and li (propriety), individuals could achieve personal and social harmony.

2. Nietzsche's Übermensch: Friedrich Nietzsche introduced the concept of the Übermensch, or "superman," as an ideal for humanity to strive towards. This vision represents a future individual who has transcended conventional morals and societal limitations to create their own values and meaning.

3. Viktor Frankl's Logotherapy: Viktor Frankl, a Holocaust survivor and psychiatrist, developed logotherapy based on the idea that the search for meaning is a primary motivational force. He argued that having a vision or ideal gives individuals a sense of purpose and helps them endure and overcome life's challenges.

Psychological Insights

The Role of Ideals in Motivation

1. Intrinsic vs. Extrinsic Motivation: Ideals often tap into intrinsic motivation, which is driven by internal satisfaction and personal fulfillment. Pursuing a vision or ideal that aligns with one's values and passions can lead to greater persistence, creativity, and overall well-being.

2. Goal-Setting Theory: Edwin Locke and Gary Latham's goal-setting theory emphasizes the importance of setting specific, challenging goals to enhance performance. Clear visions and ideals provide a sense of direction and

purpose, making it easier to develop actionable steps toward achieving them.

3. The Self-Determination Theory: This theory suggests that human beings have innate psychological needs for autonomy, competence, and relatedness. Ideals and visions often fulfill these needs by providing a sense of control over one's destiny, a challenge to develop one's abilities, and a connection to a larger purpose.

Ideals and Self-Actualization

1. Maslow's Hierarchy of Needs: According to Abraham Maslow, self-actualization represents the fulfillment of one's potential and the realization of personal ideals. This highest level of psychological development involves the pursuit of meaningful goals, personal growth, and the expression of one's true self.

2. Flow State: Mihaly Csikszentmihalyi's concept of flow describes a state of complete immersion and engagement in an activity. This state is often achieved when individuals pursue ideals that match their skills and challenge them appropriately, leading to high levels of satisfaction and achievement.

3. Positive Psychology: Positive psychology focuses on strengths, virtues, and factors that contribute to human flourishing. The pursuit of visions and ideals is central to this

field, as it promotes a sense of purpose, resilience, and overall life satisfaction.

Biblical Wisdom

"Where there is no vision, the people perish." (Proverbs 29:18)

The Bible underscores the importance of having a vision and ideals to guide our lives. Proverbs 29:18 highlights that without a vision, people lose their way and fail to reach their full potential. This verse emphasizes the necessity of having a clear sense of purpose and direction.

Biblical Examples of Vision and Ideals

1. Joseph's Dreams: In the book of Genesis, Joseph's dreams of greatness gave him a vision for his future, even when faced with adversity. His unwavering faith in his God-given vision ultimately led to his rise to power and the fulfillment of his dreams (Genesis 37-41).

2. Nehemiah's Vision for Jerusalem: Nehemiah had a vision to rebuild the walls of Jerusalem, driven by his commitment to God and his people. Despite opposition and challenges, his clear vision and dedication led to the successful completion of the project (Nehemiah 1-6).

3. Paul's Mission: The Apostle Paul had a vision of spreading the gospel to the Gentiles. His unwavering commitment to this divine mission, despite numerous trials

and persecutions, resulted in the establishment of many early Christian communities (Acts 9, 13-28).

The Role of Faith and Hope

1. Faith as Assurance: Hebrews 11:1 defines faith as "the assurance of things hoped for, the conviction of things not seen." Having a vision and ideals requires faith in their eventual realization, even when they are not immediately visible.

2. Hope as an Anchor: Hebrews 6:19 describes hope as "an anchor for the soul, firm and secure." A vision or ideal provides hope, anchoring individuals in difficult times and giving them the strength to persevere.

3. Transforming Vision into Reality: Ephesians 3:20 states, "Now to him who is able to do immeasurably more than all we ask or imagine, according to his power that is at work within us." This verse encourages believers to trust in God's ability to bring their visions and ideals to fruition.

Integrating Philosophical, Psychological, and Biblical Insights

Practical Applications

1. Define Your Vision: Reflect on your deepest values, passions, and aspirations. Create a clear and compelling vision that aligns with your beliefs and desires.

2. Visualize Success: Regularly practice visualization techniques to create a mental image of your desired outcomes. Use these images to motivate and guide your actions.

3. Set Clear Goals: Break down your vision into specific, achievable goals. Develop a step-by-step plan to reach these goals, and regularly review and adjust your progress.

4. Cultivate a Growth Mindset: Embrace challenges, learn from setbacks, and view effort as essential to achieving your ideals. Maintain a positive attitude and a willingness to grow.

5. Seek Divine Guidance: Commit your vision and goals to God, seeking His wisdom and strength. Trust in His plans and remain open to His guidance throughout your journey.

Visions and ideals are powerful forces that shape our lives, providing direction, purpose, and motivation. By integrating philosophical insights, psychological principles, and biblical wisdom, we can harness the creative power of thought to achieve our highest potential. Let us strive to define and pursue our visions and ideals, guided by faith and a commitment to personal growth, to lead fulfilling and impactful lives.

CHAPTER 11

SERENITY AND PEACE OF MIND

Serenity and peace of mind are essential for leading a balanced and fulfilling life. These states allow us to navigate challenges with equanimity, make sound decisions, and cultivate meaningful relationships. This chapter delves into the philosophical pursuit of inner peace in Buddhism and Stoicism, exploring how these traditions offer profound insights into achieving tranquility.

Philosophical Perspectives

Buddhism: The Path to Inner Peace

1. The Four Noble Truths: Central to Buddhist philosophy, the Four Noble Truths outline the nature of suffering (dukkha) and the path to its cessation. By recognizing the causes of suffering and practicing the Eightfold Path, individuals can attain inner peace. The Eightfold Path includes right understanding, intention, speech, action, livelihood, effort, mindfulness, and

concentration, each contributing to a balanced and serene mind.

2. Meditation and Mindfulness: Buddhism emphasizes meditation and mindfulness as key practices for achieving inner peace. Through meditation, individuals can calm the mind, develop insight, and cultivate compassion. Mindfulness, or the practice of being fully present in the moment, helps reduce stress and fosters a deep sense of peace and acceptance.

3. Detachment and Non-Attachment: The Buddhist concept of detachment involves letting go of attachments to desires, possessions, and outcomes. By practicing non-attachment, individuals can reduce suffering and maintain a state of inner peace, regardless of external circumstances.

Stoicism: The Pursuit of Tranquility

1. Understanding Control: Stoicism teaches that serenity comes from distinguishing between what is within our control and what is not. According to Epictetus, we should focus on our thoughts, beliefs, and actions, while accepting external events with equanimity. This understanding helps cultivate inner peace by reducing anxiety over uncontrollable factors.

2. Virtue as the Highest Good: For Stoics, living in accordance with virtue—wisdom, courage, justice, and

temperance—is the path to true tranquility. By aligning our actions with these virtues, we achieve inner harmony and peace of mind, regardless of external circumstances.

3. Accepting Fate: Stoicism advocates for amor fati, or the love of fate. This philosophy encourages embracing whatever happens in life as necessary and beneficial. By accepting and even loving our fate, we can maintain serenity and resilience in the face of adversity.

Comparative Insights

1. Mindfulness and Presence: Both Buddhism and Stoicism emphasize the importance of mindfulness and presence. While Buddhism focuses on meditation and mindfulness practices, Stoicism teaches mindful attention to one's thoughts and actions. Both traditions highlight the value of being fully present to achieve peace of mind.

2. Non-Attachment and Acceptance: Non-attachment in Buddhism and acceptance in Stoicism both contribute to inner peace. By letting go of desires and accepting the flow of life, individuals can reduce suffering and maintain tranquility.

3. Ethical Living: Both traditions advocate for ethical living as a foundation for inner peace. Buddhism's Eightfold Path and Stoicism's virtues both guide individuals toward moral integrity, which fosters a sense of peace and well-being.

Psychological Insights

Serenity and Peace of Mind in Psychology

1. Stress Reduction and Relaxation: Psychological research shows that practices such as meditation, mindfulness, and deep relaxation techniques significantly reduce stress and promote peace of mind. These practices lower cortisol levels, enhance emotional regulation, and improve overall well-being.

2. Cognitive Behavioral Techniques: Cognitive-behavioral therapy (CBT) emphasizes the role of thoughts in influencing emotions and behaviors. By identifying and challenging negative thought patterns, individuals can cultivate a more peaceful and balanced mental state.

3. Emotional Regulation: Developing skills in emotional regulation is key to maintaining serenity. Techniques such as deep breathing, progressive muscle relaxation, and mindfulness help individuals manage their emotions and respond to stressors more calmly.

Positive Psychology and Inner Peace

1. Gratitude Practices: Positive psychology highlights the benefits of gratitude in enhancing well-being and peace of mind. Regularly practicing gratitude helps shift focus from negative to positive aspects of life, fostering a sense of contentment and tranquility.

2. Strengths and Virtues: Identifying and cultivating personal strengths and virtues, as advocated by positive psychology, contributes to inner peace. By living in alignment with one's values and strengths, individuals experience greater fulfillment and serenity.

3. Mindfulness-Based Interventions: Mindfulness-based interventions, such as Mindfulness-Based Stress Reduction (MBSR) and Mindfulness-Based Cognitive Therapy (MBCT), have been shown to significantly improve mental health and promote peace of mind. These interventions teach individuals to be present, accept their experiences, and reduce reactivity to stress.

Biblical Wisdom

"Peace I leave with you; my peace I give you. I do not give to you as the world gives. Do not let your hearts be troubled and do not be afraid." (John 14:27)

The Bible emphasizes the importance of peace and offers divine guidance for achieving it. John 14:27 highlights that true peace comes from God, transcending worldly understanding and providing a deep sense of security and calm.

Biblical Examples of Serenity and Peace

1. Jesus Calming the Storm: In Mark 4:35-41, Jesus calms a storm on the Sea of Galilee, demonstrating His power

to bring peace in the midst of chaos. This story illustrates that faith in Jesus can provide inner calm, even in turbulent times.

2. Paul's Contentment: In Philippians 4:11-13, the Apostle Paul expresses his contentment in all circumstances, whether in abundance or need. His trust in Christ's strength and provision enabled him to maintain peace of mind, regardless of external conditions.

3. The Peace of God: Philippians 4:6-7 advises believers to present their requests to God with thanksgiving, promising that the peace of God, which transcends all understanding, will guard their hearts and minds in Christ Jesus. This passage emphasizes prayer and gratitude as pathways to divine peace.

The Role of Faith and Trust

1. Trusting God's Plan: Proverbs 3:5-6 encourages believers to trust in the Lord with all their heart and lean not on their own understanding. Trusting in God's plan and guidance brings a sense of peace and assurance, even when circumstances are uncertain.

2. Casting Anxieties on God: 1 Peter 5:7 advises, "Cast all your anxiety on him because he cares for you." This verse underscores the importance of entrusting our worries to God, knowing that He cares for us and provides peace.

3. Divine Presence: Psalm 23:4 reassures believers that even in the darkest valleys, they need not fear, for God is with them. His presence brings comfort and peace, guiding them through life's challenges.

Integrating Philosophical, Psychological, and Biblical Insights

Practical Applications

1. Mindfulness Practice: Incorporate mindfulness techniques such as meditation, deep breathing, and present-moment awareness into your daily routine to reduce stress and cultivate inner peace.

2. Non-Attachment and Acceptance: Practice letting go of attachments to outcomes and accepting life's circumstances with equanimity. This mindset reduces suffering and fosters serenity.

3. Trust in God: Strengthen your faith and trust in God's plan through regular prayer, meditation on Scripture, and participation in spiritual communities. Allow His peace to guard your heart and mind.

4. Gratitude Journaling: Maintain a gratitude journal to regularly reflect on and appreciate the positive aspects of your life. This practice shifts focus from negativity and promotes a peaceful, contented mindset.

5. Ethical Living: Live in accordance with your values and virtues. Ethical living not only enhances personal integrity but also contributes to inner harmony and peace of mind.

Serenity and peace of mind are achievable through the integration of philosophical wisdom, psychological practices, and biblical teachings. By embracing mindfulness, non-attachment, and trust in God, we can navigate life's challenges with equanimity and maintain a deep sense of inner peace. Let us strive to cultivate these states, allowing them to guide us toward a balanced, fulfilling, and tranquil life.

Serenity and peace of mind are crucial for a balanced and fulfilling life. They allow us to face challenges with equanimity, make sound decisions, and nurture meaningful relationships. This chapter explores psychological techniques for achieving peace of mind, such as mindfulness and meditation, and incorporates biblical wisdom to illustrate the importance of divine peace.

Psychological Techniques for Achieving Peace of Mind

Mindfulness and Meditation

1. Mindfulness: Mindfulness is the practice of being fully present and engaged in the current moment without judgment. It involves paying attention to thoughts, feelings, and sensations as they arise, allowing them to pass without

getting caught up in them. Research shows that mindfulness reduces stress, enhances emotional regulation, and improves overall well-being.

2. Meditation: Meditation is a practice where an individual uses a technique—such as focusing the mind on a particular object, thought, or activity—to achieve a mentally clear and emotionally calm state. Types of meditation include:

- Focused Attention Meditation: Concentrating on a single point of focus, such as the breath or a mantra.

- Open Monitoring Meditation: Observing all aspects of the experience without attachment.

- Loving-Kindness Meditation: Fostering feelings of compassion and love towards oneself and others.

Scientific Evidence

1. Stress Reduction: Studies have shown that mindfulness and meditation significantly reduce levels of cortisol, the stress hormone. This reduction leads to a decrease in anxiety and improved stress management.

2. Improved Emotional Regulation: Meditation practices increase awareness of one's emotional state, helping individuals respond to emotions more constructively. This enhanced emotional regulation contributes to a more stable and peaceful mind.

3. Enhanced Focus and Attention: Regular meditation improves concentration and cognitive flexibility, enabling individuals to stay focused and less distracted by external and internal disturbances.

Cognitive-Behavioral Techniques

1. Cognitive Restructuring: This technique involves identifying and challenging negative thought patterns and replacing them with more positive and realistic ones. By altering thought processes, individuals can achieve a more peaceful and balanced mental state.

2. Relaxation Techniques: Progressive muscle relaxation, deep breathing exercises, and guided imagery are effective ways to reduce physical tension and promote mental relaxation. These techniques can be integrated into daily routines to maintain a serene mind.

Positive Psychology Practices

1. Gratitude: Cultivating gratitude involves recognizing and appreciating the positive aspects of life. Practices such as keeping a gratitude journal can shift focus from negativity and foster a sense of contentment and peace.

2. Strengths and Virtues: Identifying and using personal strengths and virtues can enhance well-being and contribute to inner peace. By living in alignment with one's

core values, individuals experience greater fulfillment and serenity.

Biblical Wisdom

"Peace I leave with you; my peace I give you. I do not give to you as the world gives. Do not let your hearts be troubled and do not be afraid." (John 14:27)

The Bible offers profound insights into achieving and maintaining peace of mind. John 14:27 emphasizes that true peace comes from Jesus, providing a sense of security and calm that transcends worldly understanding.

Examples of Biblical Peace

1. Jesus Calming the Storm: In Mark 4:35-41, Jesus calms a storm, demonstrating His power to bring peace in chaotic situations. This story illustrates that faith in Jesus can provide inner calm even in turbulent times.

2. Paul's Contentment: In Philippians 4:11-13, the Apostle Paul expresses contentment in all circumstances, whether in abundance or need. His trust in Christ's strength and provision enabled him to maintain peace of mind regardless of external conditions.

3. The Peace of God: Philippians 4:6-7 advises believers to present their requests to God with thanksgiving, promising that the peace of God, which transcends all understanding, will guard their hearts and minds in Christ

Jesus. This passage emphasizes prayer and gratitude as pathways to divine peace.

Trusting God's Plan

1. Trusting in God's Sovereignty: Proverbs 3:5-6 encourages believers to trust in the Lord with all their heart and lean not on their own understanding. Trusting in God's plan brings a sense of peace and assurance, even when circumstances are uncertain.

2. Casting Anxieties on God: 1 Peter 5:7 advises, "Cast all your anxiety on him because he cares for you." This verse underscores the importance of entrusting our worries to God, knowing that He cares for us and provides peace.

3. Divine Presence: Psalm 23:4 reassures believers that even in the darkest valleys, they need not fear, for God is with them. His presence brings comfort and peace, guiding them through life's challenges.

Integrating Psychological and Biblical Insights

Practical Applications

1. Daily Mindfulness Practice: Incorporate mindfulness techniques such as meditation and deep breathing into your daily routine to reduce stress and cultivate inner peace.

2. Trust in God: Strengthen your faith and trust in God's plan through regular prayer, meditation on Scripture,

and participation in spiritual communities. Allow His peace to guard your heart and mind.

3. Gratitude Journaling: Maintain a gratitude journal to regularly reflect on and appreciate the positive aspects of your life. This practice shifts focus from negativity and promotes a peaceful, contented mindset.

4. Ethical Living: Live in accordance with your values and virtues. Ethical living not only enhances personal integrity but also contributes to inner harmony and peace of mind.

5. Emotional Regulation Techniques: Use cognitive-behavioral techniques to identify and challenge negative thought patterns, and practice relaxation techniques to manage stress effectively.

Achieving serenity and peace of mind involves a combination of psychological techniques and spiritual practices. By integrating mindfulness, meditation, and positive psychology with biblical wisdom, individuals can navigate life's challenges with equanimity and maintain a deep sense of inner peace. Let us strive to cultivate these states, allowing them to guide us toward a balanced, fulfilling, and tranquil life.

CHAPTER 12

THE LAW OF ATTRACTION

The Law of Attraction is a powerful principle suggesting that our thoughts and emotions attract corresponding experiences into our lives. This concept, deeply rooted in New Thought philosophy, posits that positive thoughts bring positive experiences, while negative thoughts attract negative outcomes. This chapter explores the philosophical underpinnings of the Law of Attraction, its applications in personal development, and how it aligns with biblical teachings.

The Principle of Attraction in New Thought Philosophy

New Thought Movement

1. Origins and Development: The New Thought movement emerged in the late 19th century, influenced by the

transcendentalist ideas of Ralph Waldo Emerson, the spiritual teachings of Phineas Quimby, and the metaphysical principles espoused by thinkers like Mary Baker Eddy and Charles Fillmore. The movement emphasizes the power of the mind in shaping reality.

2. Core Beliefs: Central to New Thought philosophy is the belief that the mind can heal the body, attract prosperity, and manifest desires. This philosophy advocates the importance of positive thinking, affirmations, and visualization in creating one's reality.

The Law of Attraction

1. Definition: The Law of Attraction is the belief that like attracts like. It suggests that our thoughts, whether positive or negative, attract corresponding events and circumstances into our lives.

2. Mechanism: The mechanism of the Law of Attraction involves focusing on desired outcomes with a positive mindset. By doing so, individuals send out vibrational energy that aligns with their desires, attracting similar energy back to them.

Philosophical Foundations

1. Emerson's Influence: Ralph Waldo Emerson, a key figure in transcendentalism, emphasized the power of thought and the interconnectedness of all things. His essays,

particularly "Self-Reliance" and "The Over-Soul," highlight the idea that individuals can shape their destiny through their thoughts and beliefs.

2. Practical Applications: New Thought practitioners advocate for daily affirmations, visualization techniques, and maintaining a positive attitude. These practices are designed to align one's thoughts with their desired reality, thereby manifesting their goals.

Psychological Insights

Cognitive-Behavioral Theory

1. Positive Thinking: Cognitive-behavioral theory (CBT) supports the idea that thoughts influence emotions and behaviors. By altering negative thought patterns and cultivating positive ones, individuals can improve their mental health and overall well-being.

2. Visualization: Visualization techniques involve imagining oneself achieving desired outcomes. This practice enhances motivation, increases self-efficacy, and primes the brain to recognize and seize opportunities.

The Power of Affirmations

1. Affirmations: Positive affirmations are statements that individuals repeat to themselves to reinforce positive beliefs and attitudes. Research shows that affirmations can reduce stress, increase resilience, and improve performance.

2. Self-Fulfilling Prophecy: The concept of self-fulfilling prophecy in psychology suggests that believing in a certain outcome can influence behaviors and attitudes in ways that make the outcome more likely to occur. This aligns with the Law of Attraction's emphasis on positive expectation.

Biblical Perspectives

Biblical Alignment with the Law of Attraction

1. Faith and Belief: The Bible emphasizes the power of faith and belief in shaping one's reality. Jesus taught that faith as small as a mustard seed can move mountains (Matthew 17:20), underscoring the profound impact of belief on outcomes.

2. Positive Confession: Proverbs 18:21 states, "The tongue has the power of life and death." This verse highlights the significance of spoken words and their ability to influence one's life, aligning with the Law of Attraction's emphasis on positive affirmations.

Examples of Biblical Attraction

1. The Woman with the Issue of Blood: In Mark 5:25-34, a woman who had been suffering from bleeding for twelve years believed that if she just touched Jesus' cloak, she would be healed. Her faith and positive expectation led to her miraculous healing.

2. Abraham's Promise: Abraham's unwavering faith in God's promise led to the fulfillment of that promise, despite seemingly insurmountable obstacles (Romans 4:18-21). His positive belief attracted the realization of God's covenant with him.

3. God's Provision: Philippians 4:19 assures believers that "God will meet all your needs according to the riches of his glory in Christ Jesus." This verse reinforces the idea that trust and belief in God's provision attract His blessings.

Integrating New Thought Philosophy and Biblical Teachings

Practical Applications

1. Daily Affirmations: Start each day with positive affirmations that align with your goals and desires. Affirmations such as "I am capable of achieving my dreams" or "God's blessings flow abundantly in my life" can set a positive tone for the day.

2. Visualization Techniques: Spend a few

minutes each day visualizing your goals and desired outcomes. Imagine yourself achieving these goals in vivid detail, experiencing the emotions and sensations associated with your success. Visualization can prime your mind for positive action and attract the circumstances needed to realize your dreams.

3. Gratitude Practice: Cultivate a habit of expressing gratitude for the blessings in your life. Keeping a gratitude journal and regularly acknowledging the good things you have can shift your focus from lack to abundance, enhancing your ability to attract more positivity.

4. Scriptural Meditation: Integrate biblical verses into your meditation and affirmation practices. Reflect on scriptures that emphasize faith, provision, and positive expectation, such as Jeremiah 29:11 or Philippians 4:19, to reinforce your belief in God's plan and provision.

5. Positive Confession: Speak positively about your life, circumstances, and future. Avoid negative self-talk and replace it with declarations of faith and optimism. Trust in the power of your words to shape your reality, as suggested in Proverbs 18:21.

The Law of Attraction, rooted in New Thought philosophy, emphasizes the power of positive thinking and belief in shaping one's reality. By integrating psychological techniques such as positive affirmations, visualization, and gratitude practices with biblical teachings on faith and provision, individuals can harness the creative power of their thoughts to attract the life they desire. Embrace the principles outlined in this chapter, and experience the transformative impact of aligning your thoughts with your highest aspirations and divine purpose.

The Law of Attraction is a principle suggesting that our thoughts and emotions attract corresponding experiences into our lives. This concept, deeply rooted in New Thought philosophy, posits that positive thoughts bring positive experiences, while negative thoughts attract negative outcomes. In this chapter, we will explore the psychological mechanisms behind the Law of Attraction and how it aligns with biblical teachings.

The Principle of Attraction in New Thought Philosophy

New Thought Movement

1. Origins and Development: The New Thought movement emerged in the late 19th century, influenced by the transcendentalist ideas of Ralph Waldo Emerson, the spiritual teachings of Phineas Quimby, and the metaphysical principles espoused by thinkers like Mary Baker Eddy and Charles Fillmore. The movement emphasizes the power of the mind in shaping reality.

2. Core Beliefs: Central to New Thought philosophy is the belief that the mind can heal the body, attract prosperity, and manifest desires. This philosophy advocates the

importance of positive thinking, affirmations, and visualization in creating one's reality.

The Law of Attraction

1. Definition: The Law of Attraction is the belief that like attracts like. It suggests that our thoughts, whether positive or negative, attract corresponding events and circumstances into our lives.

2. Mechanism: The mechanism of the Law of Attraction involves focusing on desired outcomes with a positive mindset. By doing so, individuals send out vibrational energy that aligns with their desires, attracting similar energy back to them.

Psychological Insights

Cognitive-Behavioral Theory

1. Positive Thinking: Cognitive-behavioral theory (CBT) supports the idea that thoughts influence emotions and behaviors. By altering negative thought patterns and cultivating positive ones, individuals can improve their mental health and overall well-being.

2. Visualization: Visualization techniques involve imagining oneself achieving desired outcomes. This practice enhances motivation, increases self-efficacy, and primes the brain to recognize and seize opportunities.

The Power of Affirmations

1. Affirmations: Positive affirmations are statements that individuals repeat to themselves to reinforce positive beliefs and attitudes. Research shows that affirmations can reduce stress, increase resilience, and improve performance.

2. Self-Fulfilling Prophecy: The concept of self-fulfilling prophecy in psychology suggests that believing in a certain outcome can influence behaviors and attitudes in ways that make the outcome more likely to occur. This aligns with the Law of Attraction's emphasis on positive expectation.

Psychoneuroimmunology

1. Mind-Body Connection: Psychoneuroimmunology explores how thoughts and emotions influence the immune system and overall physical health. Positive thinking and a hopeful outlook can enhance immune function and promote healing, while chronic stress and negative emotions can weaken the immune system.

2. Stress Reduction: Techniques such as mindfulness, meditation, and positive visualization can reduce stress and improve physical health. By focusing on positive outcomes and maintaining a hopeful mindset, individuals can support their body's natural healing processes.

Biblical Perspectives

Biblical Alignment with the Law of Attraction

1. Faith and Belief: The Bible emphasizes the power of faith and belief in shaping one's reality. Jesus taught that faith as small as a mustard seed can move mountains (Matthew 17:20), underscoring the profound impact of belief on outcomes.

2. Positive Confession: Proverbs 18:21 states, "The tongue has the power of life and death." This verse highlights the significance of spoken words and their ability to influence one's life, aligning with the Law of Attraction's emphasis on positive affirmations.

Examples of Biblical Attraction

1. The Woman with the Issue of Blood: In Mark 5:25-34, a woman who had been suffering from bleeding for twelve years believed that if she just touched Jesus' cloak, she would be healed. Her faith and positive expectation led to her miraculous healing.

2. Abraham's Promise: Abraham's unwavering faith in God's promise led to the fulfillment of that promise, despite seemingly insurmountable obstacles (Romans 4:18-21). His positive belief attracted the realization of God's covenant with him.

3. God's Provision: Philippians 4:19 assures believers that "God will meet all your needs according to the riches of

his glory in Christ Jesus." This verse reinforces the idea that trust and belief in God's provision attract His blessings.

Jesus' Teaching on Belief and Prayer

Mark 11:24 encapsulates the essence of the Law of Attraction: "Therefore I tell you, whatever you ask for in prayer, believe that you have received it, and it will be yours." Jesus highlights the importance of belief in receiving what we ask for. This principle aligns perfectly with the Law of Attraction, which posits that belief and expectation are crucial in manifesting desires.

Integrating New Thought Philosophy and Biblical Teachings

Practical Applications

1. Daily Affirmations: Start each day with positive affirmations that align with your goals and desires. Affirmations such as "I am capable of achieving my dreams" or "God's blessings flow abundantly in my life" can set a positive tone for the day.

2. Visualization Techniques: Spend a few minutes each day visualizing your goals and desired outcomes. Imagine yourself achieving these goals in vivid detail, experiencing the emotions and sensations associated with your success. Visualization can prime your mind for positive action and attract the circumstances needed to realize your dreams.

3. Gratitude Practice: Cultivate a habit of expressing gratitude for the blessings in your life. Keeping a gratitude journal and regularly acknowledging the good things you have can shift your focus from lack to abundance, enhancing your ability to attract more positivity.

4. Scriptural Meditation: Integrate biblical verses into your meditation and affirmation practices. Reflect on scriptures that emphasize faith, provision, and positive expectation, such as Jeremiah 29:11 or Philippians 4:19, to reinforce your belief in God's plan and provision.

5. Positive Confession: Speak positively about your life, circumstances, and future. Avoid negative self-talk and replace it with declarations of faith and optimism. Trust in the power of your words to shape your reality, as suggested in Proverbs 18:21.

The Law of Attraction, rooted in New Thought philosophy, emphasizes the power of positive thinking and belief in shaping one's reality. By integrating psychological techniques such as positive affirmations, visualization, and gratitude practices with biblical teachings on faith and provision, individuals can harness the creative power of their thoughts to attract the life they desire. Embrace the principles outlined in this chapter, and experience the transformative impact of aligning your thoughts with your highest aspirations and divine purpose.

CHAPTER 13

MENTAL RESILIENCE

Mental resilience is the ability to withstand and recover from adversity, stress, and life's challenges. It is a crucial attribute for maintaining mental health and achieving long-term success. This chapter explores the concept of resilience through the lens of Stoic philosophy, providing insights into how ancient wisdom can help us develop the inner strength to navigate life's difficulties.

Stoic Philosophy on Resilience

Origins of Stoicism

1. Founders and Influencers: Stoicism was founded in the early 3rd century BCE by Zeno of Citium. Key figures in the development of Stoic philosophy include Seneca, Epictetus, and Marcus Aurelius, whose teachings continue to influence modern thought on resilience and personal fortitude.

2. Core Principles: Stoicism emphasizes the importance of rationality, self-control, and virtue in achieving a tranquil and resilient mind. It teaches that while we cannot control external events, we can control our responses to them.

Resilience in Stoic Philosophy

1. Control and Acceptance: One of the central tenets of Stoicism is the dichotomy of control, which distinguishes between what we can control (our thoughts, actions, and reactions) and what we cannot control (external events and other people's actions). By focusing on what we can control and accepting what we cannot, we cultivate resilience.

2. Perception and Interpretation: Stoics believe that adversity is not inherently negative; it is our perception and interpretation of events that determine our emotional response. Marcus Aurelius wrote, "The impediment to action advances action. What stands in the way becomes the way." This perspective encourages us to see obstacles as opportunities for growth.

3. Virtue and Character: Stoicism teaches that true resilience comes from developing virtues such as wisdom, courage, justice, and temperance. By embodying these virtues, we build a strong character capable of facing adversity with grace and fortitude.

Psychological Insights into Resilience

Cognitive-Behavioral Approaches

1. Reframing Negative Thoughts: Cognitive-behavioral therapy (CBT) aligns with Stoic principles by emphasizing the importance of reframing negative thoughts. By challenging and changing unhelpful thinking patterns, individuals can build resilience and improve their emotional well-being.

2. Stress Management Techniques: Techniques such as mindfulness, deep breathing, and progressive muscle relaxation can help manage stress and enhance resilience. These practices enable individuals to remain calm and composed in the face of adversity.

Positive Psychology

1. Growth Mindset: A growth mindset, as proposed by Carol Dweck, is the belief that abilities and intelligence can be developed through effort and perseverance. This mindset fosters resilience by encouraging individuals to view challenges as opportunities for learning and growth.

2. Gratitude and Optimism: Cultivating gratitude and maintaining an optimistic outlook are key components of resilience. Research shows that gratitude can enhance well-being and buffer against stress, while optimism promotes a positive approach to life's challenges.

Building Resilience

1. Self-Efficacy: Belief in one's ability to handle challenges is a crucial aspect of resilience. Developing self-efficacy through setting and achieving small goals can build confidence and resilience over time.

2. Social Support: Strong social connections provide emotional support and practical assistance during difficult times. Building and maintaining supportive relationships can enhance resilience by providing a network of resources and encouragement.

Biblical Perspectives on Resilience

Faith and Perseverance

1. Trusting God's Plan: The Bible teaches that resilience is rooted in faith and trust in God's plan. Romans 8:28 assures believers that "in all things, God works for the good of those who love him." This verse encourages a perspective of trust and hope in the face of adversity.

2. Perseverance through Trials: James 1:2-4 states, "Consider it pure joy, my brothers and sisters, whenever you face trials of many kinds, because you know that the testing of your faith produces perseverance. Let perseverance finish its work so that you may be mature and complete, not lacking anything." This passage highlights the transformative power of enduring trials with faith.

Biblical Examples of Resilience

1. Job's Endurance: The story of Job is a profound example of resilience in the Bible. Despite losing his wealth, health, and family, Job remained faithful to God and eventually saw his fortunes restored. His story teaches the importance of unwavering faith and perseverance in the face of immense suffering.

2. Paul's Trials: The Apostle Paul faced numerous hardships, including imprisonment, beatings, and shipwrecks, yet he remained steadfast in his mission to spread the gospel. In Philippians 4:13, he writes, "I can do all this through him who gives me strength," demonstrating his reliance on God's strength to endure adversity.

3. Jesus' Teachings on Resilience: Jesus taught about resilience and the importance of building one's life on a solid foundation. In Matthew 7:24-25, he says, "Therefore everyone who hears these words of mine and puts them into practice is like a wise man who built his house on the rock. The rain came down, the streams rose, and the winds blew and beat against that house; yet it did not fall, because it had its foundation on the rock." This parable underscores the importance of faith and obedience in developing resilience.

Practical Applications

1. Daily Reflection: Spend time each day reflecting on your thoughts and actions. Identify areas where you can apply

Stoic principles, such as focusing on what you can control and reframing negative perceptions.

2. Mindfulness Practice: Incorporate mindfulness practices into your daily routine. Techniques such as meditation, deep breathing, and progressive muscle relaxation can help manage stress and enhance resilience.

3. Gratitude Journaling: Keep a gratitude journal to regularly acknowledge the blessings in your life. Focusing on positive aspects can shift your mindset from lack to abundance, enhancing your resilience.

4. Scriptural Study: Integrate biblical verses into your daily reflections. Meditate on scriptures that emphasize faith, perseverance, and trust in God's plan to reinforce your resilience.

5. Building Social Support: Strengthen your social connections by investing in relationships that provide emotional support and encouragement. Engage in activities that foster community and build a network of resources for challenging times.

Resilience, as explored through Stoic philosophy, psychological insights, and biblical teachings, is a vital attribute for navigating life's adversities. By embracing the principles of rationality, self-control, and virtue from Stoicism, integrating psychological techniques such as mindfulness and positive thinking, and grounding our resilience in faith and trust in God's plan, we can develop the mental fortitude to face challenges with grace and strength. Embrace the strategies outlined in this chapter to cultivate resilience and experience the transformative power of a resilient mind and spirit.

Mental resilience refers to the capacity to withstand adversity, bounce back from challenges, and maintain a sense of well-being in the face of stress and trauma. This chapter explores psychological theories of resilience, coping mechanisms, and how biblical wisdom can provide strength and support during difficult times.

Psychological Theories of Resilience

1. The Resilience Theory

Resilience Theory focuses on the processes and mechanisms through which individuals adapt positively despite experiencing significant adversity. Key components of this theory include:

- Protective Factors: These are conditions or attributes that help individuals manage stress and reduce the impact of adversity. Examples include supportive relationships, a positive self-concept, and problem-solving skills.

- Risk Factors: These are conditions or variables associated with a higher likelihood of negative outcomes.

Understanding these factors can help in developing interventions to bolster resilience.

2. The Biopsychosocial Model

The Biopsychosocial Model posits that resilience is influenced by a complex interplay of biological, psychological, and social factors. This model emphasizes that:

- Biological Factors: Genetic predispositions and neurobiological responses can affect an individual's ability to cope with stress.

- Psychological Factors: Cognitive processes, emotional regulation, and personality traits play a crucial role in resilience.

- Social Factors: Social support, cultural influences, and community resources are vital for fostering resilience.

3. The Positive Psychology Approach

Positive Psychology focuses on strengths, virtues, and factors that contribute to a fulfilling life. It emphasizes the importance of:

- Optimism: Maintaining a hopeful outlook can enhance resilience by encouraging individuals to see challenges as opportunities for growth.

- Gratitude: Recognizing and appreciating positive aspects of life can buffer against stress and improve mental well-being.

- Meaning and Purpose: Having a sense of purpose can provide motivation and direction, helping individuals to persevere through adversity.

Coping Mechanisms

1. Problem-Focused Coping

Problem-focused coping involves actively addressing the source of stress to reduce its impact. Strategies include:

- Problem-Solving: Identifying solutions and taking actionable steps to resolve issues.

- Time Management: Organizing and prioritizing tasks to manage workload and reduce stress.

2. Emotion-Focused Coping

Emotion-focused coping aims to manage emotional responses to stress. Techniques include:

- Mindfulness and Meditation: Practicing mindfulness can help individuals stay present and reduce anxiety.

- Expressive Writing: Writing about thoughts and feelings can provide emotional release and clarity.

3. Social Support

Seeking and maintaining social connections can provide emotional and practical support during challenging times. Strategies include:

- Building Relationships: Investing in meaningful relationships that offer mutual support.

- Joining Support Groups: Participating in groups where individuals can share experiences and offer encouragement.

4. Cognitive Restructuring

Cognitive restructuring involves identifying and changing negative thought patterns. Techniques include:

- Cognitive-Behavioral Therapy (CBT): CBT helps individuals recognize and challenge distorted thoughts, replacing them with more constructive ones.

- Positive Self-Talk: Encouraging oneself with affirmations and positive statements can boost confidence and resilience.

Biblical Wisdom on Resilience

Faith as a Source of Strength

1. Philippians 4:13: "I can do all this through him who gives me strength." This verse emphasizes the power of faith in providing strength and resilience. Believers can draw upon their faith to navigate life's challenges with confidence and perseverance.

2. Isaiah 40:31: "But those who hope in the Lord will renew their strength. They will soar on wings like eagles; they will run and not grow weary, they will walk and not be faint." Trusting in God's support and guidance can renew one's strength and resilience.

Perseverance and Hope

1. James 1:2-4: "Consider it pure joy, my brothers and sisters, whenever you face trials of many kinds, because you know that the testing of your faith produces perseverance. Let perseverance finish its work so that you may be mature and complete, not lacking anything." Trials and challenges are opportunities for growth and the development of resilience.

2. Romans 5:3-5: "Not only so, but we also glory in our sufferings, because we know that suffering produces perseverance; perseverance, character; and character, hope. And hope does not put us to shame, because God's love has been poured out into our hearts through the Holy Spirit, who has been given to us." This passage highlights the transformative power of enduring hardships with faith, leading to the development of character and hope.

Practical Applications

1. Daily Prayer and Meditation: Incorporate prayer and meditation into your daily routine to strengthen your connection with God and cultivate inner peace.

2. Scripture Study: Regularly study and reflect on biblical verses that emphasize resilience and perseverance.

3. Community Involvement: Engage in community activities and build supportive relationships within your faith community.

Mental resilience is a multifaceted concept that involves the ability to adapt and thrive despite adversity. By integrating psychological theories, coping mechanisms, and biblical wisdom, individuals can develop the inner strength needed to navigate life's challenges. Embracing resilience not only enhances personal well-being but also provides a foundation for achieving long-term success and fulfillment.

CHAPTER 14

THE POWER OF POSITIVE THINKING

Positive thinking is a mental attitude that emphasizes optimism and constructive perspectives. This chapter explores the philosophical foundations of positive thinking in the works of Descartes and Spinoza and delves into how these ideas can be applied to foster a more fulfilling and resilient life.

Philosophical Underpinnings of Positive Thinking

Descartes: The Power of Rational Thought

René Descartes, a prominent French philosopher, is often referred to as the father of modern philosophy. His emphasis on the power of rational thought laid the groundwork for positive thinking in several ways:

1. Cogito, Ergo Sum ("I think, therefore I am"): Descartes' famous declaration underscores the fundamental role of thought in defining our existence. By acknowledging

the power of our thoughts, we can recognize their influence on our reality.

2. Rational Optimism: Descartes believed in the ability of human reason to solve problems and improve the human condition. This rational optimism encourages a positive outlook, suggesting that through clear and logical thinking, we can overcome challenges and enhance our lives.

3. Mind-Body Dualism: Descartes posited that the mind and body are distinct entities. This separation implies that while our physical circumstances may be challenging, our mental state can remain positive and influential in shaping our experiences.

Spinoza: The Ethics of Positive Thinking

Baruch Spinoza, a Dutch philosopher, contributed significantly to the philosophy of positive thinking through his work "Ethics." Spinoza's ideas emphasize the importance of aligning our thoughts with reality to achieve a state of well-being:

1. Determinism and Acceptance: Spinoza argued that everything in the universe follows a predetermined order. Understanding and accepting this can lead to a more positive outlook, as we recognize that our emotions and experiences are part of a larger, rational system.

2. Power of the Mind: Spinoza believed that by understanding the nature of reality and our place within it, we can achieve a state of "blessedness" or happiness. This involves cultivating a positive mindset and focusing on constructive, rational thoughts.

3. Emotional Regulation: Spinoza's philosophy highlights the importance of regulating emotions through reason. By understanding the causes of our emotions, we can transform negative feelings into positive ones, leading to greater emotional stability and resilience.

Applications of Positive Thinking

1. Rational Problem-Solving

- Logical Analysis: Apply Descartes' method of systematic doubt and logical analysis to identify and solve problems. Break down complex issues into smaller, manageable parts and address them methodically.

- Constructive Solutions: Focus on finding constructive solutions rather than dwelling on problems. This approach promotes a positive and proactive mindset.

2. Acceptance and Realism

- Realistic Optimism: Embrace Spinoza's idea of determinism by accepting the reality of your circumstances. Cultivate a realistic optimism that balances hope with an understanding of the limitations and possibilities of the situation.

- Mindfulness: Practice mindfulness to stay present and accept each moment as it is. This can help reduce anxiety and promote a positive outlook.

3. Emotional Transformation

- Emotional Awareness: Increase your awareness of your emotions and their triggers. By understanding the root causes of negative emotions, you can work towards transforming them into positive ones.

- Positive Reframing: Reframe negative experiences in a positive light. Look for lessons and opportunities for growth in every situation.

Biblical Wisdom on Positive Thinking

The Bible provides numerous teachings that align with the principles of positive thinking:

1. Philippians 4:8: "Finally, brothers and sisters, whatever is true, whatever is noble, whatever is right, whatever is pure, whatever is lovely, whatever is admirable—if anything is excellent or praiseworthy—think about such things." This verse encourages focusing on positive and virtuous thoughts, which can lead to a more fulfilling and joyful life.

2. Proverbs 17:22: "A cheerful heart is a good medicine, but a crushed spirit dries up the bones." A positive and cheerful attitude can have a profound impact on physical and mental health.

3. Romans 12:2: "Do not conform to the pattern of this world, but be transformed by the renewing of your mind." Renewing the mind through positive thinking can lead to a transformative and fulfilling life.

Practical Applications

1. Daily Affirmations: Incorporate positive affirmations into your daily routine to reinforce a positive mindset.

2. Gratitude Practice: Regularly reflect on and express gratitude for the positive aspects of your life.

3. Positive Environment: Surround yourself with positive influences, including supportive people, inspiring literature, and uplifting activities.

The power of positive thinking, rooted in the philosophies of Descartes and Spinoza, and reinforced by biblical wisdom, offers a pathway to a more resilient and fulfilling life. By cultivating a positive mindset, embracing rational problem-solving, and transforming negative emotions, individuals can navigate life's challenges with grace and optimism.

Positive thinking is more than just a catchphrase; it's a mental attitude that has profound impacts on our overall mental health and well-being. In this chapter, we will delve into the psychological benefits of positive thinking, supported by empirical research, and explore how maintaining a positive mindset can lead to a healthier, more fulfilling life. We will also reflect on the biblical wisdom found in Philippians 4:8, which emphasizes the importance of focusing on what is good and virtuous.

Psychological Benefits of Positive Thinking

1. Enhanced Mental Health

Positive thinking significantly contributes to mental health by reducing the prevalence of mental health issues such as depression and anxiety. Here are a few ways positive thinking can improve mental health:

- Reduced Stress Levels: Positive thinkers tend to have lower levels of stress hormones, which can mitigate the physical and emotional impacts of stress. They view stressful situations as challenges to overcome rather than threats, which can lead to more effective stress management.

- Improved Mood: Focusing on positive thoughts and experiences can elevate mood and foster a sense of well-being. Positive thinking promotes the release of neurotransmitters like serotonin and dopamine, which are associated with happiness and pleasure.

2. Better Physical Health

The mind and body are interconnected, and positive thinking can have tangible effects on physical health:

- Stronger Immune System: Studies have shown that individuals with a positive outlook tend to have stronger immune responses. Positive emotions can boost the body's resistance to illnesses.

- Lower Blood Pressure: Positive thinking is linked to lower blood pressure, which reduces the risk of heart disease and stroke.

- Increased Longevity: Optimistic individuals often live longer, healthier lives. A positive mindset encourages healthy behaviors such as regular exercise, a balanced diet, and adequate sleep.

3. Enhanced Coping Skills

Positive thinking enhances one's ability to cope with adversity. Optimistic individuals are more likely to:

- Seek Solutions: Rather than dwelling on problems, positive thinkers focus on finding solutions. This proactive approach can lead to better outcomes in difficult situations.

- Build Resilience: Positive thinking fosters resilience, enabling individuals to bounce back from setbacks and maintain a sense of purpose and direction.

4. Improved Relationships

A positive outlook can improve interpersonal relationships:

- Better Communication: Positive thinkers are more likely to engage in constructive communication and express gratitude and appreciation, which strengthens relationships.

- Social Support: Optimistic individuals often attract and maintain supportive social networks, which can provide emotional and practical support during challenging times.

5. Enhanced Performance

Positive thinking can boost performance in various aspects of life, including work, academics, and personal pursuits:

- Increased Motivation: A positive mindset can enhance motivation and perseverance, leading to greater achievement and success.

- Improved Problem-Solving: Optimistic individuals approach problems with creativity and confidence, leading to more effective solutions.

Biblical Wisdom on Positive Thinking

The Bible offers profound insights into the power of positive thinking. Philippians 4:8 is a powerful verse that encourages believers to focus on what is good and virtuous:

Philippians 4:8: "Finally, brothers and sisters, whatever is true, whatever is noble, whatever is right, whatever is pure, whatever is lovely, whatever is admirable—if anything is excellent or praiseworthy—think about such things."

This verse emphasizes the importance of directing our thoughts towards positive and virtuous subjects. By focusing on what is true, noble, right, pure, lovely, and admirable, we can cultivate a mindset that is aligned with God's will and conducive to mental and emotional well-being.

1. True and Noble Thoughts

Focusing on what is true and noble encourages us to:

- Seek Truth: Embrace honesty and integrity in our thoughts and actions.

- Uphold Virtue: Aspire to live by high moral standards and principles.

2. Right and Pure Thoughts

Directing our thoughts towards what is right and pure helps us to:

- Cultivate Righteousness: Strive for justice and fairness in our dealings with others.

- Maintain Purity: Guard our hearts and minds against negative influences and sinful thoughts.

3. Lovely and Admirable Thoughts

Thinking about what is lovely and admirable inspires us to:

- Appreciate Beauty: Recognize and appreciate the beauty in God's creation and in the people around us.

- Pursue Excellence: Aim for excellence in all we do, seeking to glorify God through our efforts.

4. Excellent and Praiseworthy Thoughts

Focusing on what is excellent and praiseworthy encourages us to:

- Celebrate Goodness: Recognize and celebrate the goodness in our lives and the lives of others.

- Praise God: Offer praise and gratitude to God for His blessings and His presence in our lives.

Practical Applications of Positive Thinking

1. Daily Gratitude Practice: Take time each day to reflect on and write down things you are grateful for. This can shift your focus from negative to positive aspects of your life.

2. Positive Affirmations: Use positive affirmations to reinforce a positive self-image and mindset. Repeat phrases such as "I am capable," "I am loved," and "I can overcome challenges."

3. Mindfulness and Meditation: Practice mindfulness and meditation to stay present and focused on positive thoughts. This can help reduce stress and increase overall well-being.

4. Surround Yourself with Positivity: Build a positive environment by surrounding yourself with supportive and optimistic people, engaging in uplifting activities, and consuming inspiring content.

The power of positive thinking is a transformative force that can enhance mental and physical health, improve relationships, and boost overall well-being. By aligning our thoughts with the principles found in Philippians 4:8 and embracing a positive mindset, we can navigate life's challenges with resilience and grace. Positive thinking is not about ignoring reality or avoiding difficulties but about approaching life with a constructive and hopeful attitude that fosters growth and fulfillment.

CHAPTER 15

THE ROLE OF FAITH

Faith is a fundamental aspect of human existence that has been explored by philosophers for centuries. It intersects with reason, challenging us to consider how beliefs formed beyond empirical evidence can shape our lives and our understanding of the world. This chapter delves into the philosophical exploration of faith and reason, examining how these concepts coexist and influence one another.

The Intersection of Faith and Reason in Philosophy

Philosophy has long grappled with the relationship between faith and reason. These two dimensions of human thought, though sometimes seen as opposing forces, can also be viewed as complementary. Philosophers such as Thomas Aquinas, Immanuel Kant, and Søren Kierkegaard have offered profound insights into this dynamic interplay.

1. Thomas Aquinas: Harmonizing Faith and Reason

Thomas Aquinas, a medieval philosopher and theologian, is renowned for his efforts to reconcile faith and reason. In his seminal work, Summa Theologica, Aquinas argued that faith and reason are not mutually exclusive but rather work together to lead us to truth. According to Aquinas:

- Natural Theology: Aquinas believed that reason could lead us to certain truths about God through the study of nature and the use of logic. This approach, known as natural theology, posits that evidence of God can be found in the natural world.

- Revealed Theology: Faith, on the other hand, provides access to divine truths that are beyond the reach of reason alone. These truths are revealed through scripture and the teachings of the Church.

Aquinas maintained that while reason can guide us to certain understandings of God, faith completes our knowledge by revealing deeper spiritual truths.

2. Immanuel Kant: The Limits of Reason

Immanuel Kant, an Enlightenment philosopher, explored the limits of reason and the necessity of faith in understanding certain aspects of human existence. In his Critique of Pure Reason, Kant argued that:

- Phenomena and Noumena: Human knowledge is limited to phenomena, the world as we experience it through our senses. The noumenal world, or the realm of things-in-themselves, lies beyond our sensory experience and comprehension.

- Moral Faith: Kant introduced the concept of "moral faith," asserting that belief in God, freedom, and immortality is necessary to make sense of our moral experience. While these beliefs cannot be proven through reason alone, they provide a framework for understanding moral obligations and the pursuit of virtue.

Kant's philosophy highlights the role of faith in providing meaning and coherence to our moral and existential inquiries, even when empirical evidence is lacking.

3. Søren Kierkegaard: Faith as a Leap

Søren Kierkegaard, a 19th-century Danish philosopher, is often regarded as the father of existentialism. He emphasized the subjective and personal nature of faith, describing it as a "leap" beyond rational evidence. According to Kierkegaard:

- Subjective Truth: Faith is a deeply personal and subjective experience that involves a commitment to something greater than oneself. It cannot be fully explained or justified through objective reasoning.

- Leap of Faith: Kierkegaard introduced the concept of the "leap of faith," wherein an individual embraces belief in God despite the absence of empirical proof. This leap requires courage and involves a recognition of the limitations of human reason.

Kierkegaard's existential approach underscores the transformative power of faith as a personal and passionate commitment that shapes one's identity and purpose.

The Role of Faith in Shaping Beliefs and Actions

Faith plays a critical role in shaping our beliefs and actions. It provides a sense of purpose, guides moral decisions, and offers comfort in times of uncertainty. Here are a few ways in which faith influences our lives:

1. Providing Purpose and Meaning

Faith often serves as a foundation for understanding the meaning and purpose of life. It offers answers to existential questions and provides a framework for interpreting the world and our place within it. Whether through religious belief or personal philosophy, faith can inspire individuals to live with intentionality and direction.

2. Guiding Moral Decisions

Faith-based principles often inform ethical behavior and decision-making. Many religious traditions provide moral guidelines that help individuals navigate complex moral dilemmas. Even outside of religious contexts, faith in certain values and ideals can drive ethical conduct.

3. Offering Comfort and Hope

Faith can provide solace and hope during difficult times. Believing in a higher power or a greater plan can offer comfort and resilience in the face of adversity. This sense of hope can be a powerful motivator, helping individuals to persevere and maintain a positive outlook.

Biblical Perspective on Faith

The Bible offers profound insights into the nature and importance of faith. One of the most significant biblical passages on faith is found in Hebrews 11:1:

Hebrews 11:1: "Now faith is confidence in what we hope for and assurance about what we do not see."

This verse highlights the essence of faith as both a confident expectation and a firm belief in the unseen. The Bible provides numerous examples of individuals whose faith enabled them to overcome challenges and achieve great things. Here are a few key lessons from the Bible on the role of faith:

1. Faith as Trust in God

Faith involves trusting in God's promises and His plan for our lives. Abraham is often cited as a model of faith in the Bible. Despite not knowing where he was going, Abraham trusted God's promise and set out on a journey that would establish him as the father of many nations (Hebrews 11:8-10).

2. Faith in Action

True faith is demonstrated through actions. The Epistle of James emphasizes that faith without deeds is dead (James 2:17). Genuine faith manifests in how we live our lives and how we treat others, reflecting our beliefs through our actions.

3. Faith Amidst Adversity

The Bible also teaches that faith is particularly important during times of hardship. The story of Job illustrates unwavering faith amidst suffering. Despite losing everything, Job maintained his faith in God, ultimately experiencing restoration and blessings (Job 42:10-17).

The role of faith in our lives is profound and multifaceted. Philosophically, it bridges the gap between reason and the transcendent, offering a framework for understanding aspects of existence that lie beyond empirical evidence. Psychologically, faith provides meaning, guides ethical behavior, and offers comfort in times of distress. Biblically, faith is depicted as a confident trust in God and His promises, exemplified through the lives of individuals who relied on their faith to navigate life's challenges.

By exploring the intersection of faith and reason, we gain a deeper appreciation of how these elements coexist and shape our understanding of the world. Faith, in its various forms, continues to be a powerful force that influences our beliefs, actions, and ultimately, our lives.

Faith is an integral component of human existence that significantly impacts our mental and emotional well-being. This chapter explores the psychological dimensions of faith and spirituality, examining how they contribute to our overall well-being. Drawing from various psychological theories and biblical wisdom, we delve into the ways faith influences our minds and hearts.

The Psychological Impact of Faith and Spirituality on Well-Being

Psychological research has consistently demonstrated that faith and spirituality can have profound effects on an individual's mental health and overall well-being. Here, we explore several key areas where faith contributes to psychological resilience and happiness.

1. Faith as a Source of Comfort and Hope

Faith provides individuals with a sense of comfort and hope, especially during times of stress or adversity. Belief in a higher power or a greater plan can help people find meaning in difficult circumstances, which is essential for psychological resilience.

- Stress Reduction: Studies have shown that individuals with strong spiritual beliefs tend to experience lower levels of stress and anxiety. This is often due to the comforting belief that they are not alone and that their struggles have a purpose.

- Hope and Optimism: Faith fosters a hopeful outlook on life. People who believe in a benevolent higher power are more likely to maintain a positive attitude and expect good outcomes, which can enhance their overall sense of well-being.

2. Faith and Coping Mechanisms

Faith-based coping mechanisms are strategies that individuals use to deal with life's challenges. These can include prayer, meditation, and participation in religious communities.

- Prayer and Meditation: Engaging in prayer or meditation can provide a sense of calm and focus, reducing feelings of anxiety and depression. These practices allow individuals to express their concerns and seek guidance, which can be therapeutic.

- Community Support: Being part of a faith community offers social support, which is crucial for mental health. Regular interaction with like-minded individuals can provide a sense of belonging and emotional support, helping people to cope with life's challenges.

3. Faith and Purpose in Life

Faith often gives individuals a sense of purpose and direction, which is vital for psychological well-being.

- Meaning and Purpose: Having a sense of purpose is associated with higher levels of happiness and life satisfaction. Faith can provide a framework for understanding one's place in the world and one's role in a larger plan, which can be deeply fulfilling.

- Goal Setting and Motivation: Faith can inspire individuals to set and pursue meaningful goals. Believing that one's actions have a higher purpose can motivate people to strive for excellence and persevere in the face of obstacles.

4. Faith and Moral Development

Faith influences moral development and ethical behavior, shaping how individuals interact with others and make decisions.

- Moral Guidance: Many religious traditions offer clear moral guidelines, which can help individuals make ethical decisions and develop a strong sense of right and wrong. This moral clarity can contribute to a stable and coherent sense of self.

- Altruism and Compassion: Faith often encourages altruistic behavior and compassion towards others. Engaging in acts of kindness and service can enhance one's self-esteem and foster a sense of community and connection.

5. Psychological Theories on Faith and Well-Being

Several psychological theories provide insights into the relationship between faith and well-being.

- Positive Psychology: This field emphasizes the study of positive emotions, strengths, and virtues. Faith and spirituality are often associated with positive psychological outcomes, such as increased happiness, greater life satisfaction, and reduced rates of depression.

- Attachment Theory: This theory explores the bonds we form with caregivers in early life and how these bonds affect our relationships and sense of security. For many, faith functions as an attachment figure, providing a secure base and a source of comfort and support.

- Cognitive Behavioral Therapy (CBT): CBT focuses on the relationship between thoughts, emotions, and behaviors. Faith can influence cognitive processes by promoting positive thinking patterns, reducing negative self-talk, and encouraging a more hopeful and optimistic outlook.

Biblical Perspective on Faith

The Bible offers profound insights into the nature and significance of faith. One of the most illuminating verses is found in Hebrews 11:1:

Hebrews 11:1: "Now faith is confidence in what we hope for and assurance about what we do not see."

This verse encapsulates the essence of faith as both a confident expectation and a firm belief in the unseen. It highlights the transformative power of faith, which is evident in the lives of many biblical figures who relied on their faith to navigate life's challenges.

1. Faith as Trust in God's Promises

The Bible portrays faith as a deep trust in God's promises. For example, Abraham's unwavering faith in God's promise led him to leave his homeland and journey to an unknown land, demonstrating profound trust and obedience (Hebrews 11:8-10).

2. Faith in Action

True faith is reflected in actions. The Epistle of James emphasizes that faith without deeds is dead (James 2:17). Genuine faith manifests in how we live our lives, making decisions that align with our beliefs and values.

3. Faith Amidst Adversity

Faith is particularly vital during times of adversity. The story of Job illustrates unwavering faith amidst suffering.

Despite losing everything, Job maintained his faith in God, ultimately experiencing restoration and blessings (Job 42:10-17).

The role of faith in our lives is multifaceted and profound. Psychologically, faith provides comfort, hope, and a sense of purpose, contributing significantly to mental and emotional well-being. It offers coping mechanisms, moral guidance, and a supportive community, enhancing resilience and fostering a positive outlook on life.

Biblically, faith is depicted as a confident trust in God's promises, exemplified through the lives of individuals who relied on their faith to navigate life's challenges. By understanding the psychological and biblical dimensions of faith, we gain a deeper appreciation of its transformative power and its essential role in shaping our beliefs, actions, and overall well-being.

CHAPTER 16

OVERCOMING NEGATIVE THOUGHTS

Negative thoughts are a universal human experience, often acting as significant barriers to personal growth and happiness. From a philosophical standpoint, particularly within existentialism, overcoming negativity involves confronting the inherent challenges and uncertainties of life with a proactive and resilient mindset. This chapter explores the existential perspective on overcoming negativity, examining how embracing existential principles can help transform our mental landscapes.

Existentialism and the Human Condition

Existentialism, a philosophical movement that emerged in the 19th and 20th centuries, focuses on the individual's experience of existence and the meaning of life. Prominent existentialists like Søren Kierkegaard, Jean-Paul Sartre, and Friedrich Nietzsche have explored themes of anxiety, freedom, and the search for meaning. Understanding their perspectives provides valuable insights into overcoming negative thoughts.

1. The Absurd and Meaning-Making

Existentialists often discuss the concept of the "absurd," the inherent meaninglessness of life in the face of an indifferent universe. According to existential thought, individuals must create their own meaning and purpose.

- Albert Camus: In "The Myth of Sisyphus," Camus describes the absurd hero who, despite the futility of his task, finds meaning in his struggle. Overcoming negativity involves recognizing life's absurdity and choosing to persist and find personal significance in our actions.

2. Freedom and Responsibility

Existentialism emphasizes individual freedom and the responsibility that comes with it. Negative thoughts often stem from feelings of powerlessness and lack of control.

- Jean-Paul Sartre: Sartre's notion of "existence precedes essence" suggests that individuals are free to define their own existence through their choices. Overcoming negativity involves embracing this freedom and accepting responsibility for our actions and attitudes.

3. Authenticity and Self-Discovery

Existentialists advocate for living authentically, true to one's values and beliefs, rather than conforming to societal expectations.

- Søren Kierkegaard: Kierkegaard emphasized the importance of personal choice and commitment in living an authentic life. Overcoming negativity requires a journey of self-discovery, where individuals identify and align with their true selves, leading to greater fulfillment and resilience.

The Existential Approach to Overcoming Negativity

Drawing from existential principles, several strategies can help individuals overcome negative thoughts and foster a more positive and authentic existence.

1. Embrace the Absurd

Recognizing the inherent uncertainties and challenges of life can be liberating. By acknowledging the absurd, individuals can shift their focus from seeking external validation to creating their own meaning.

- Finding Meaning in Struggle: Like Camus's Sisyphus, finding personal meaning in our efforts and challenges can transform our perspective. Viewing obstacles as opportunities for growth and self-discovery can help mitigate negative thoughts.

2. Exercise Freedom and Responsibility

Accepting that we have the freedom to choose our responses to situations empowers us to overcome negativity.

- Empowerment Through Choice: By making conscious choices that align with our values and goals, we reclaim control over our lives. This proactive stance can reduce feelings of helplessness and promote a more positive outlook.

3. Cultivate Authenticity

Living authentically involves understanding and expressing our true selves, rather than conforming to external pressures.

- Self-Reflection and Commitment: Regular self-reflection helps individuals identify their core values and beliefs. Committing to living in accordance with these principles fosters a sense of purpose and resilience against negative thoughts.

4. Engage in Existential Reflection

Existential reflection involves contemplating fundamental questions about existence, purpose, and personal values.

- Journaling and Meditation: Practices like journaling and meditation can facilitate existential reflection. By exploring our thoughts and emotions, we can gain deeper insights into our negative patterns and develop strategies for overcoming them.

Biblical Perspective on Overcoming Negative Thoughts

The Bible offers profound wisdom on overcoming negative thoughts, emphasizing the power of faith, gratitude, and positive thinking. One key verse that speaks to this theme is found in Philippians 4:8:

Philippians 4:8: "Finally, brothers and sisters, whatever is true, whatever is noble, whatever is right, whatever is pure, whatever is lovely, whatever is admirable—if anything is excellent or praiseworthy—think about such things."

This verse highlights the importance of focusing on positive and uplifting thoughts, encouraging believers to cultivate a mindset centered on goodness and virtue.

1. Renewing the Mind

The Bible encourages believers to renew their minds, transforming their thinking patterns to align with God's truth.

- Romans 12:2: "Do not conform to the pattern of this world, but be transformed by the renewing of your mind." Renewing the mind involves replacing negative thoughts with positive, faith-filled perspectives, fostering mental and emotional well-being.

2. Casting Out Fear and Anxiety

Scripture offers reassurance and comfort, urging believers to cast their fears and anxieties onto God.

- 1 Peter 5:7: "Cast all your anxiety on him because he cares for you." Trusting in God's care and provision can alleviate negative thoughts and promote a sense of peace and security.

3. Embracing Gratitude

Gratitude is a powerful antidote to negativity. The Bible encourages believers to cultivate a thankful heart.

- 1 Thessalonians 5:18: "Give thanks in all circumstances; for this is God's will for you in Christ Jesus." Practicing gratitude shifts our focus from what is lacking to what we have, fostering a positive and contented mindset.

Overcoming negative thoughts is a multifaceted process that involves philosophical introspection, practical strategies, and spiritual wisdom. Existentialism provides valuable insights into embracing life's challenges, exercising freedom and responsibility, and living authentically. Biblical teachings offer guidance on renewing the mind, casting out fear, and embracing gratitude.

By integrating these philosophical and spiritual principles, individuals can develop resilience, find meaning in their struggles, and cultivate a positive and fulfilling mental landscape. Embracing the journey of overcoming negativity not only enhances personal well-being but also empowers us to lead more authentic and purpose-driven lives.

Negative thoughts can significantly impact our mental health and overall well-being. They can create a cycle of anxiety, depression, and stress, making it difficult to lead a fulfilling life. Cognitive-behavioral strategies offer practical tools for managing these thoughts effectively. This chapter explores cognitive-behavioral techniques to overcome negative thinking, complemented by the profound wisdom found in biblical scripture.

Cognitive-Behavioral Strategies for Managing Negative Thoughts

Cognitive-behavioral therapy (CBT) is a well-established psychological approach that focuses on identifying and changing negative thought patterns. The core principle of CBT is that our thoughts, feelings, and behaviors are interconnected, and by altering our thoughts, we can influence our emotions and actions.

1. Identifying Negative Thoughts

The first step in CBT is to become aware of negative thoughts. These thoughts are often automatic and can go unnoticed, yet they profoundly affect our mood and behavior.

- Mindfulness and Self-Monitoring: Practicing mindfulness helps individuals become more aware of their thoughts and emotions in the present moment. Keeping a thought diary can also be useful in identifying recurring negative thoughts and patterns.

2. Challenging Negative Thoughts

Once negative thoughts are identified, the next step is to challenge their validity. This involves questioning the evidence for and against these thoughts.

Cognitive Restructuring: This technique helps individuals evaluate the accuracy of their thoughts. For example, if someone thinks, "I am a failure," they are encouraged to examine the evidence supporting and contradicting this belief. This process helps to create a more balanced and realistic perspective.

3. Replacing Negative Thoughts

After challenging negative thoughts, the goal is to replace them with more positive and constructive ones.

- Positive Affirmations and Reframing: Using positive affirmations can help reinforce new, healthier thought patterns. Reframing involves looking at situations from a different perspective, focusing on positive aspects or potential opportunities for growth.

4. Behavioral Activation

Negative thoughts often lead to avoidance behaviors, which can reinforce the cycle of negativity. Behavioral activation aims to counteract this by encouraging engagement in positive and rewarding activities.

- Activity Scheduling: Planning and engaging in activities that bring joy and a sense of accomplishment can help improve mood and reduce negative thinking.

5. Relaxation Techniques

Stress and anxiety often accompany negative thoughts. Learning relaxation techniques can help manage these feelings and create a more positive mental state.

- Deep Breathing and Progressive Muscle Relaxation: These techniques promote physical relaxation, which can help calm the mind and reduce the intensity of negative thoughts.

Biblical Perspective on Overcoming Negative Thoughts

The Bible provides timeless wisdom for managing negative thoughts, emphasizing the importance of faith, prayer, and gratitude. One key verse that addresses this issue is Philippians 4:6:

Philippians 4:6: "Do not be anxious about anything, but in every situation, by prayer and petition, with thanksgiving, present your requests to God."

This verse highlights several important principles for overcoming negative thoughts.

1. Do Not Be Anxious

The Bible encourages us not to be anxious, reminding us that we can trust in God's provision and care.

- Trust in God's Promises: Reflecting on God's promises and His faithfulness can provide comfort and reduce anxiety. Knowing that we are not alone in our struggles can help us manage negative thoughts more effectively.

2. Prayer and Petition

Turning to prayer allows us to bring our concerns to God, seeking His guidance and support.

- The Power of Prayer: Regular prayer helps cultivate a deeper relationship with God, providing a sense of peace and assurance. Prayer can also serve as a form of cognitive restructuring, helping us to reframe our thoughts in the context of faith.

3. With Thanksgiving

Gratitude is a powerful tool for combating negativity. Focusing on what we are thankful for shifts our attention away from negative thoughts.

- Cultivating Gratitude: Keeping a gratitude journal can help us regularly reflect on and acknowledge the positive aspects of our lives. This practice can significantly improve our overall mental outlook.

Integrating CBT and Biblical Principles

Combining cognitive-behavioral strategies with biblical principles can provide a holistic approach to overcoming negative thoughts.

1. Trusting in God's Plan

Understanding that God has a plan for our lives, as mentioned in Jeremiah 29:11, can help us reframe negative thoughts and trust that challenges have a purpose.

Jeremiah 29:11: "For I know the plans I have for you, declares the Lord, plans to prosper you and not to harm you, plans to give you hope and a future."

2. Seeking Strength Through Christ

Drawing strength from our faith in Christ can empower us to face and overcome negative thoughts.

Philippians 4:13: "I can do all this through him who gives me strength."

3. Focusing on the Positive

Following the guidance of Philippians 4:8, we can train our minds to dwell on positive and uplifting thoughts.

Philippians 4:8: "Finally, brothers and sisters, whatever is true, whatever is noble, whatever is right, whatever is pure, whatever is lovely, whatever is admirable—

if anything is excellent or praiseworthy—think about such things."

Overcoming negative thoughts requires a multifaceted approach that addresses both the cognitive and spiritual aspects of our lives. Cognitive-behavioral strategies provide practical tools for identifying, challenging, and replacing negative thoughts, while biblical principles offer profound spiritual support and guidance. By integrating these approaches, we can cultivate a more positive and resilient mindset, ultimately leading to greater mental and emotional well-being.

CHAPTER 17

THE INFLUENCE OF SOCIETY

The thoughts and beliefs of individuals are significantly shaped by the society in which they live. Social contract theory, proposed by philosophers like Thomas Hobbes, John Locke, and Jean-Jacques Rousseau, provides a framework for understanding the relationship between individuals and their societies. This chapter explores how societal norms and structures influence individual thought from a philosophical perspective.

Social Contract Theory: An Overview

Social contract theory posits that individuals come together to form societies through implicit agreements or contracts. These agreements establish the rules and norms that govern social behavior, creating order and facilitating cooperation. In return, individuals receive protection and the benefits of living in an organized community.

Thomas Hobbes: In his work "Leviathan," Hobbes argued that in the state of nature, life was "solitary, poor, nasty, brutish, and short." To escape this chaotic state, individuals collectively agreed to surrender some of their freedoms to a sovereign authority in exchange for security and order.

John Locke: Locke's perspective, outlined in "Two Treatises of Government," emphasized the protection of natural rights—life, liberty, and property. He believed that governments are formed to protect these rights and that individuals have the right to overthrow governments that fail to do so.

Jean-Jacques Rousseau: In "The Social Contract," Rousseau introduced the concept of the "general will," the collective desire of all citizens for the common good. He argued that true freedom is found in adherence to laws that individuals collectively create.

The Impact of Society on Individual Thought

Social contract theory highlights the influence of societal structures on individual thought and behavior. This influence can be seen in various aspects of life, including moral values, cultural norms, and political beliefs.

1. Moral Values and Ethics

Society plays a crucial role in shaping our understanding of right and wrong. Moral values are often derived from the collective beliefs and traditions of a community.

- Cultural Relativism: Different societies have unique moral codes, which can lead to varying interpretations of ethical behavior. What is considered virtuous in one culture may be seen as immoral in another.

2. Cultural Norms and Practices

Cultural norms dictate acceptable behavior within a society. These norms are learned through socialization and are reinforced by institutions such as family, education, and media.

- Socialization: From a young age, individuals are taught the norms and values of their society through interactions with family, peers, and educators. This process shapes our perceptions and behaviors.

3. Political Beliefs and Ideologies

Political systems and ideologies influence how individuals think about governance, justice, and individual rights.

- Political Socialization: Political beliefs are often influenced by factors such as education, media, and personal experiences. These beliefs shape how individuals view authority, power, and their role within the society.

Biblical Perspective on the Influence of Society

The Bible also addresses the influence of society on individual thought and behavior, emphasizing the need to discern and sometimes resist societal pressures.

Romans 12:2: "Do not conform to the pattern of this world, but be transformed by the renewing of your mind. Then you will be able to test and approve what God's will is— his good, pleasing, and perfect will."

This verse underscores the importance of critical thinking and spiritual discernment in the face of societal influences.

1. Discernment and Nonconformity

The Bible encourages believers to be discerning and not to conform blindly to societal norms that contradict God's principles.

- Critical Thinking: Developing a critical mindset allows individuals to evaluate societal norms and make decisions based on their faith and values rather than societal pressures.

2. The Role of the Church

The church serves as a countercultural community that provides support and guidance for believers to live according to biblical principles.

- Community Support: Being part of a faith community can help individuals resist negative societal influences and stay grounded in their beliefs.

3. Influencing Society for Good

Believers are called to be "salt and light" in the world, influencing society positively by living out their faith.

- Positive Impact: By embodying biblical values, individuals can challenge and transform societal norms, promoting justice, compassion, and integrity.

Integrating Philosophical and Biblical Perspectives

Integrating the insights from social contract theory with biblical principles offers a comprehensive understanding of how society influences individual thought and how individuals can navigate these influences.

1. Understanding Societal Influence

Recognizing the ways in which society shapes our thoughts and behaviors is the first step toward developing a more autonomous and authentic self.

- Awareness: By becoming aware of societal influences, individuals can critically evaluate and choose which norms and values to adopt.

2. Embracing Transformative Thinking

The Bible's call to be transformed by the renewing of our minds aligns with the philosophical idea of self-actualization and authenticity.

- Personal Growth: Embracing a transformative mindset allows individuals to grow and develop in alignment with their true values and beliefs.

3. Engaging with Society

Believers are encouraged to engage with society thoughtfully and intentionally, seeking to make a positive impact while staying true to their faith.

- Constructive Engagement: By engaging with societal issues from a place of faith and critical thinking, individuals can contribute to the common good and promote positive change.

The influence of society on individual thought is profound and multifaceted. Social contract theory provides valuable insights into how societal structures shape our beliefs and behaviors. At the same time, biblical principles offer guidance on how to navigate these influences with discernment and integrity. By integrating these perspectives, individuals can develop a more balanced and thoughtful approach to engaging with society, ultimately leading to a more fulfilling and authentic life.

Society plays a significant role in shaping individual thoughts, beliefs, and behaviors. Social psychology examines how societal norms and influences affect our thinking processes. This chapter delves into the psychological mechanisms underlying societal influence and integrates biblical wisdom to understand how we can navigate and transform these influences.

Social Psychology and Societal Norms

Social psychology is the scientific study of how individuals think, feel, and behave in social contexts. One of its key areas of focus is understanding how societal norms influence individual behavior and thought processes.

1. Social Norms and Conformity

Social norms are the unwritten rules and expectations about how people should behave in particular social groups or cultures. These norms exert a powerful influence on individual behavior and thought.

- Conformity: Conformity refers to the act of matching attitudes, beliefs, and behaviors to group norms. Solomon Asch's famous conformity experiments demonstrated how individuals often conform to group opinions, even when those opinions are clearly incorrect.

- Peer Pressure: The desire to fit in and be accepted by others can lead individuals to adopt behaviors and beliefs that align with the majority, sometimes against their better judgment.

2. Social Identity and Group Membership

Our sense of self is heavily influenced by the groups we belong to, whether they are based on family, culture, religion, or social interests.

- Social Identity Theory: Proposed by Henri Tajfel and John Turner, this theory suggests that a person's self-concept is derived from perceived membership in social groups. This identification can strongly influence attitudes and behaviors.

- Ingroup and Outgroup Dynamics: Individuals tend to favor members of their own groups (ingroup) and may exhibit bias against those outside their groups (outgroup). This dynamic can shape perceptions and reinforce societal norms.

3. The Role of Culture

Culture encompasses the beliefs, behaviors, objects, and other characteristics shared by groups of people. It is a central concept in social psychology because it profoundly influences how we think and act.

- Cultural Conditioning: From a young age, individuals are conditioned to adopt the values and norms of their culture. This conditioning shapes their worldview and behavior patterns.

- Cross-Cultural Differences: Understanding how different cultures influence thinking and behavior is crucial for appreciating the diversity of human experience. What is considered normal in one culture may be viewed differently in another.

Biblical Perspective on Societal Influence

The Bible provides guidance on how to navigate societal influences, emphasizing the importance of discernment and transformation through the renewal of the mind.

Romans 12:2: "Do not conform to the pattern of this world, but be transformed by the renewing of your mind. Then you will be able to test and approve what God's will is— his good, pleasing and perfect will."

This verse underscores the necessity of resisting conformity to worldly patterns and seeking transformation through spiritual renewal.

1. Discernment and Nonconformity

The Bible encourages believers to be discerning and not to conform blindly to societal norms that contradict God's principles.

- Critical Thinking: Developing a critical mindset allows individuals to evaluate societal norms and make decisions based on their faith and values rather than societal pressures.

- Spiritual Guidance: Seeking guidance through prayer and scripture can help believers discern God's will and navigate societal influences.

2. The Role of the Faith Community

The church and faith communities provide support and guidance for believers to live according to biblical principles.

- Community Support: Being part of a faith community can help individuals resist negative societal influences and stay grounded in their beliefs. The community offers a counterbalance to societal pressures, reinforcing positive values and behaviors.

- Accountability: Within a faith community, members hold each other accountable, encouraging one another to live out their faith authentically and resist conforming to harmful societal norms.

3. Influencing Society for Good

Believers are called to be "salt and light" in the world, influencing society positively by living out their faith.

- Positive Impact: By embodying biblical values, individuals can challenge and transform societal norms, promoting justice, compassion, and integrity. This transformative influence can help reshape societal structures to reflect more closely the principles of God's kingdom.

Integrating Psychological and Biblical Perspectives

Combining insights from social psychology with biblical teachings offers a comprehensive understanding of how societal norms influence thought and behavior and how individuals can navigate these influences faithfully.

1. Awareness and Reflection

Understanding the mechanisms of social influence helps individuals become more aware of how their thoughts and behaviors are shaped by society.

- Self-Reflection: Reflecting on personal beliefs and behaviors in light of social influences allows individuals to identify areas where they may be conforming to societal norms that conflict with their values.

- Mindfulness: Practicing mindfulness helps individuals remain present and conscious of societal pressures, enabling them to respond thoughtfully rather than reactively.

2. Embracing Transformative Thinking

The biblical call to renew our minds aligns with the psychological principles of cognitive restructuring, where individuals challenge and change unhelpful thought patterns.

- Cognitive Restructuring: Techniques from cognitive-behavioral therapy (CBT) can help individuals identify and change negative thought patterns influenced by societal norms.

Spiritual Renewal: Engaging in spiritual practices such as prayer, meditation, and studying scripture fosters a renewed mind aligned with God's will.

3. Engaging Society Constructively

Believers are encouraged to engage with society thoughtfully and intentionally, seeking to make a positive impact while staying true to their faith.

- Constructive Engagement: By engaging with societal issues from a place of faith and critical thinking, individuals can contribute to the common good and promote positive change. This involves advocating for justice, compassion, and integrity in all areas of life.

Society profoundly influences individual thought and behavior through norms, cultural conditioning, and social identity. Social psychology provides valuable insights into these mechanisms, while biblical teachings offer guidance on how to navigate and transform societal influences. By integrating these perspectives, individuals can develop a more balanced and thoughtful approach to engaging with society, ultimately leading to a more fulfilling and authentic life.

CHAPTER 18

THE QUEST FOR TRUTH

The quest for truth is a fundamental pursuit in philosophy, psychology, and theology. It underpins our understanding of reality, shapes our beliefs, and guides our actions. This chapter delves into the philosophical exploration of truth through the works of Descartes and Kant, examines psychological insights on truth-seeking, and integrates biblical perspectives to provide a holistic view of this vital pursuit.

Philosophical Perspectives on Truth

Philosophers have long grappled with the nature of truth and how we can attain it. René Descartes and Immanuel Kant are two influential thinkers whose works offer profound insights into the quest for truth.

1. René Descartes: Methodical Doubt and Certainty

René Descartes, often considered the father of modern philosophy, embarked on a rigorous quest for certainty. His approach, known as methodical doubt, involved questioning all beliefs to establish which ones could be known with absolute certainty.

- Cogito, Ergo Sum: Descartes' famous dictum, "Cogito, ergo sum" ("I think, therefore I am"), marks the starting point of his search for indubitable truth. This statement reflects his belief that the act of thinking is undeniable proof of one's existence.

- Foundationalism: Descartes sought to build a foundation of knowledge upon clear and distinct ideas that are self-evident and certain. His meditations explore the nature of existence, the reality of the external world, and the existence of God.

2. Immanuel Kant: The Limits of Human Understanding

Immanuel Kant's philosophy revolutionized the understanding of truth and knowledge by addressing the limitations of human cognition.

- Critique of Pure Reason: In this seminal work, Kant argues that human understanding is limited by the structures of our own minds. He posits that while we can know phenomena (the world as we experience it), we cannot have direct knowledge of noumena (things-in-themselves).

- Synthetic A Priori Judgments: Kant introduces the concept of synthetic a priori judgments—statements that are necessarily true and inform our understanding of the world, such as those found in mathematics and the principles of causality.

Psychological Insights on Truth-Seeking

From a psychological perspective, the quest for truth involves cognitive processes, biases, and the impact of belief systems on perception and understanding.

1. Cognitive Processes in Truth-Seeking

The human mind employs various cognitive processes in the search for truth, including critical thinking, reasoning, and evidence evaluation.

- Critical Thinking: Critical thinking involves analyzing, evaluating, and synthesizing information to form a reasoned judgment. It is essential for distinguishing truth from falsehood.

- Cognitive Biases: Biases such as confirmation bias (favoring information that confirms existing beliefs) and availability heuristics (relying on immediate examples) can distort our perception of truth. Awareness of these biases is crucial for objective truth-seeking.

2. The Role of Belief Systems

Belief systems significantly influence how we perceive and interpret truth. Psychological studies show that deeply held beliefs can shape our understanding of reality.

- Belief Perseverance: Once beliefs are formed, they tend to persist even in the face of contradictory evidence. This phenomenon highlights the challenge of altering established beliefs.

- Cognitive Dissonance: When confronted with information that conflicts with existing beliefs, individuals experience cognitive dissonance, a state of mental discomfort. Resolving this dissonance often involves either changing beliefs or dismissing the new information.

Biblical Perspective on the Quest for Truth

The Bible offers profound wisdom on the nature of truth and the pursuit of understanding. Biblical teachings emphasize the importance of seeking truth through God's revelation.

1. The Source of Truth

The Bible identifies God as the ultimate source of truth. Jesus Christ, in particular, is portrayed as embodying truth.

- John 14:6: Jesus said, "I am the way, the truth, and the life. No one comes to the Father except through me." This verse underscores the centrality of Christ in the pursuit of truth.

- Psalm 119:160: "All your words are true; all your righteous laws are eternal." Scripture is presented as a reliable source of divine truth.

2. Seeking and Living the Truth

Believers are encouraged to seek truth diligently and to live in accordance with it.

- Proverbs 23:23: "Buy the truth and do not sell it— wisdom, instruction and insight as well." This verse highlights the value of truth and the importance of acquiring it.

- Ephesians 4:15: "Instead, speaking the truth in love, we will grow to become in every respect the mature body of him who is the head, that is, Christ." This verse emphasizes the practice of truth in love and its role in spiritual growth.

Integrating Philosophical, Psychological, and Biblical Insights

Combining insights from philosophy, psychology, and biblical teachings provides a comprehensive approach to the quest for truth.

1. Philosophical Rigorous Inquiry

Philosophy encourages rigorous inquiry and critical thinking in the search for truth. The works of Descartes and

Kant provide frameworks for understanding the complexities of truth and knowledge.

- Methodical Doubt and Certainty: Emulating Descartes' methodical doubt can help individuals scrutinize their beliefs and seek foundational truths.

- Understanding Limits: Recognizing the limits of human cognition, as Kant suggests, can foster humility and openness to continuous learning.

2. Psychological Objectivity and Awareness

Psychological principles highlight the importance of objectivity and awareness of cognitive biases in truth-seeking.

- Critical Thinking Skills: Developing critical thinking skills can enhance the ability to evaluate information and form reasoned judgments.

- Bias Awareness: Understanding and mitigating cognitive biases can lead to more accurate perceptions of truth.

3. Biblical Faith and Revelation

Biblical teachings emphasize faith and divine revelation as essential components of the quest for truth.

- Divine Guidance: Seeking truth through prayer and scripture invites divine guidance and revelation, aligning personal understanding with God's truth.

- Living Truthfully: Applying biblical principles of truth in daily life fosters integrity, authenticity, and spiritual growth.

The quest for truth is a multifaceted journey that encompasses philosophical inquiry, psychological understanding, and spiritual discernment. By integrating these perspectives, individuals can pursue truth with greater depth and clarity, ultimately leading to a more meaningful and authentic existence.

The quest for truth is a fundamental endeavor that has captivated human minds for centuries. It is an exploration that cuts across various domains of knowledge—philosophy, psychology, and theology—each offering unique insights into the nature of truth and the means to attain it. This chapter delves into philosophical perspectives, examines the role of critical thinking in discerning truth from a psychological standpoint, and integrates biblical wisdom to provide a comprehensive understanding of this vital pursuit.

Philosophical Perspectives on Truth

Philosophers have long grappled with the nature of truth and how we can attain it. Two influential thinkers, René Descartes and Immanuel Kant, offer profound insights into the quest for truth.

1. René Descartes: Methodical Doubt and Certainty

René Descartes, often considered the father of modern philosophy, embarked on a rigorous quest for certainty. His approach, known as methodical doubt, involved questioning all beliefs to establish which ones could be known with absolute certainty.

- Cogito, Ergo Sum: Descartes' famous dictum, "Cogito, ergo sum" ("I think, therefore I am"), marks the starting point of his search for indubitable truth. This statement reflects his belief that the act of thinking is undeniable proof of one's existence.

- Foundationalism: Descartes sought to build a foundation of knowledge upon clear and distinct ideas that are self-evident and certain. His meditations explore the nature of existence, the reality of the external world, and the existence of God.

2. Immanuel Kant: The Limits of Human Understanding

Immanuel Kant's philosophy revolutionized the understanding of truth and knowledge by addressing the limitations of human cognition.

- Critique of Pure Reason: In this seminal work, Kant argues that human understanding is limited by the structures of our own minds. He posits that while we can know phenomena (the world as we experience it), we cannot have direct knowledge of noumena (things-in-themselves).

- Synthetic A Priori Judgments: Kant introduces the concept of synthetic a priori judgments—statements that are necessarily true and inform our understanding of the world, such as those found in mathematics and the principles of causality.

Psychological Insights: The Role of Critical Thinking in Discerning Truth

From a psychological perspective, the quest for truth involves cognitive processes, biases, and the impact of belief systems on perception and understanding. Critical thinking is paramount in this endeavor.

1. The Importance of Critical Thinking

Critical thinking is the disciplined process of actively analyzing, evaluating, and synthesizing information gathered from observation, experience, reflection, reasoning, or communication.

- Analytical Skills: Critical thinking involves breaking down complex information into smaller parts to understand it better. This analytical approach helps in discerning truth from falsehood.

- Evaluation and Reflection: Critical thinkers evaluate evidence, examine arguments, and reflect on their own thought processes. This self-reflection is crucial for identifying biases and improving decision-making.

2. Overcoming Cognitive Biases

Cognitive biases can distort our perception of truth. Critical thinking helps mitigate these biases, leading to more objective and accurate conclusions.

- Confirmation Bias: This bias involves favoring information that confirms pre-existing beliefs while disregarding contradictory evidence. Critical thinking encourages the consideration of all relevant information, regardless of personal beliefs.

- Availability Heuristic: This heuristic relies on immediate examples that come to mind when evaluating a specific topic or decision. Critical thinking promotes the use of comprehensive evidence rather than relying on readily available information.

3. Developing Critical Thinking Skills

Enhancing critical thinking skills involves continuous practice and the application of specific strategies.

- Questioning Assumptions: Critical thinkers routinely question their assumptions and the assumptions of others. This practice prevents taking information at face value and promotes deeper understanding.

- Seeking Diverse Perspectives: Exposing oneself to diverse viewpoints fosters a more well-rounded understanding of issues and reduces the risk of echo chambers.

Biblical Perspective on the Quest for Truth

The Bible offers profound wisdom on the nature of truth and the pursuit of understanding. Biblical teachings emphasize the importance of seeking truth through God's revelation.

1. The Source of Truth

The Bible identifies God as the ultimate source of truth. Jesus Christ, in particular, is portrayed as embodying truth.

- John 14:6: Jesus said, "I am the way, the truth, and the life. No one comes to the Father except through me." This verse underscores the centrality of Christ in the pursuit of truth.

- Psalm 119:160: "All your words are true; all your righteous laws are eternal." Scripture is presented as a reliable source of divine truth.

2. Seeking and Living the Truth

Believers are encouraged to seek truth diligently and to live in accordance with it.

- John 8:32: "Then you will know the truth, and the truth will set you free." This verse highlights the liberating power of truth and the importance of seeking it earnestly.

- Proverbs 23:23: "Buy the truth and do not sell it—wisdom, instruction, and insight as well." This verse emphasizes the value of truth and the commitment required to acquire it.

Integrating Philosophical, Psychological, and Biblical Insights

Combining insights from philosophy, psychology, and biblical teachings provides a comprehensive approach to the quest for truth.

1. Philosophical Rigorous Inquiry

Philosophy encourages rigorous inquiry and critical thinking in the search for truth. The works of Descartes and Kant provide frameworks for understanding the complexities of truth and knowledge.

- Methodical Doubt and Certainty: Emulating Descartes' methodical doubt can help individuals scrutinize their beliefs and seek foundational truths.

- Understanding Limits: Recognizing the limits of human cognition, as Kant suggests, can foster humility and openness to continuous learning.

2. Psychological Objectivity and Awareness

Psychological principles highlight the importance of objectivity and awareness of cognitive biases in truth-seeking.

- Critical Thinking Skills: Developing critical thinking skills can enhance the ability to evaluate information and form reasoned judgments.

- Bias Awareness: Understanding and mitigating cognitive biases can lead to more accurate perceptions of truth.

3. Biblical Faith and Revelation

Biblical teachings emphasize faith and divine revelation as essential components of the quest for truth.

- Divine Guidance: Seeking truth through prayer and scripture invites divine guidance and revelation, aligning personal understanding with God's truth.

- Living Truthfully: Applying biblical principles of truth in daily life fosters integrity, authenticity, and spiritual growth.

The quest for truth is a multifaceted journey that encompasses philosophical inquiry, psychological understanding, and spiritual discernment. By integrating these perspectives, individuals can pursue truth with greater depth and clarity, ultimately leading to a more meaningful and authentic existence. The words of Jesus in John 8:32 remind us of the profound impact that knowing the truth can have on our lives: "Then you will know the truth, and the truth will set you free."

291

CHAPTER 19

THE IMPACT OF GRATITUDE

Gratitude, a universal virtue, has been cherished across various philosophical traditions for centuries. Recognized for its profound impact on human well-being and social harmony, gratitude transcends cultural and temporal boundaries. This chapter explores the philosophical underpinnings of gratitude from ancient to modern perspectives, delving into how this simple yet powerful practice can transform our lives.

Gratitude in Ancient Philosophy

1. Aristotle and the Virtue of Gratitude

Aristotle, one of the most influential philosophers of ancient Greece, emphasized the importance of gratitude as a fundamental virtue within his ethical framework.

- Nicomachean Ethics: In his work "Nicomachean Ethics," Aristotle identifies gratitude as a crucial element of moral character. He argues that gratitude fosters social bonds and mutual respect, which are essential for a flourishing society.

- Reciprocity: Aristotle views gratitude as part of the broader concept of reciprocity. He posits that expressing gratitude for kindness received encourages the continuation of benevolent actions, thus promoting a cycle of goodness.

2. Stoicism and the Practice of Gratitude

The Stoic philosophers, particularly Seneca and Epictetus, also highlighted the significance of gratitude.

- Seneca's Letters: In his "Letters to Lucilius," Seneca discusses the importance of being grateful for what we have, regardless of external circumstances. He believes that gratitude is a key component of a contented life.

- Epictetus' Enchiridion: Epictetus teaches that gratitude should be cultivated for everything, including challenges and hardships. According to Stoic philosophy, adopting an attitude of gratitude helps individuals maintain inner tranquility and resilience.

Gratitude in Modern Philosophy

1. Immanuel Kant and the Moral Duty of Gratitude

Immanuel Kant, an 18th-century German philosopher, viewed gratitude as a moral duty intrinsic to human relationships.

- The Metaphysics of Morals: In this work, Kant categorizes gratitude as a duty of virtue. He argues that failing to express gratitude for benefits received is morally wrong, as it undermines the reciprocal nature of social interactions.

- Respect and Gratitude: For Kant, gratitude is not merely a passive feeling but an active expression of respect and recognition for others' goodwill. It is an ethical obligation that sustains a moral community.

2. Modern Existentialism and Gratitude

Modern existentialist thinkers, such as Jean-Paul Sartre and Albert Camus, explore the concept of gratitude from the perspective of individual existence and freedom.

- Jean-Paul Sartre: While Sartre is known for his emphasis on individual freedom and responsibility, his existentialist philosophy implicitly recognizes the importance of gratitude. Sartre suggests that acknowledging the contributions of others enriches our own experience of freedom and authenticity.

- Albert Camus: Camus, in his exploration of the absurd, highlights gratitude as a response to the beauty and meaning found in life's fleeting moments. Embracing gratitude allows individuals to find joy and purpose despite life's inherent challenges.

Psychological Insights on Gratitude

1. The Positive Psychology of Gratitude

Positive psychology, a branch of psychology that focuses on strengths and virtues, has extensively studied the impact of gratitude on mental health and well-being.

- Emotional Benefits: Research indicates that practicing gratitude enhances positive emotions such as joy, contentment, and hope. It reduces negative emotions like envy, resentment, and depression.

- Social Benefits: Gratitude strengthens social bonds by promoting prosocial behaviors such as generosity, empathy, and forgiveness. Expressing gratitude fosters a sense of connection and belonging within communities.

2. Gratitude Interventions

Psychological studies have developed various interventions to cultivate gratitude, demonstrating significant benefits.

- Gratitude Journaling: Keeping a gratitude journal, where individuals regularly write down things they are thankful for, has been shown to increase overall well-being and life satisfaction.

- Gratitude Letters: Writing and delivering letters of gratitude to significant individuals in one's life can enhance both the writer's and recipient's happiness and strengthen relational bonds.

Biblical Perspective on Gratitude

The Bible places a strong emphasis on the importance of gratitude, presenting it as a fundamental aspect of spiritual life and a reflection of one's relationship with God.

1. Thanksgiving as Worship

Gratitude in the Bible is closely linked with worship and acknowledging God's goodness.

- 1 Thessalonians 5:18: "Give thanks in all circumstances; for this is God's will for you in Christ Jesus." This verse underscores the importance of maintaining a thankful heart in all situations as an expression of faith and trust in God's plan.

- Psalm 100:4: "Enter his gates with thanksgiving and his courts with praise; give thanks to him and praise his name." Gratitude is presented as an essential part of worship, inviting believers to approach God with a heart full of thankfulness.

2. Gratitude and Contentment

The Bible teaches that gratitude fosters contentment and wards off feelings of envy and discontent.

- Philippians 4:6-7: "Do not be anxious about anything, but in every situation, by prayer and petition, with thanksgiving, present your requests to God. And the peace of God, which transcends all understanding, will guard your hearts and your minds in Christ Jesus." This passage highlights the role of gratitude in achieving inner peace and contentment.

- 1 Timothy 6:6-8: "But godliness with contentment is great gain. For we brought nothing into the world, and we can take nothing out of it. But if we have food and clothing, we will be content with that." Gratitude for basic necessities fosters a sense of contentment and reduces materialistic desires.

Integrating Philosophical, Psychological, and Biblical Insights

Combining insights from philosophy, psychology, and biblical teachings provides a comprehensive understanding of gratitude and its transformative power.

1. Philosophical Reflection and Moral Duty

Philosophy encourages deep reflection on the nature and importance of gratitude, presenting it as both a virtue and a moral duty.

- Virtue and Reciprocity: Reflecting on Aristotle's and Kant's teachings can inspire individuals to cultivate gratitude as a key aspect of moral character and social harmony.

- Existential Embrace: Existentialist perspectives highlight the importance of embracing gratitude as a way to find meaning and joy in life's complexities.

2. Psychological Practice and Well-being

Psychological research provides practical strategies for cultivating gratitude and demonstrates its profound impact on mental and emotional well-being.

- Gratitude Exercises: Engaging in gratitude journaling and other interventions can enhance positive emotions, strengthen social connections, and improve overall life satisfaction.

- Mental Health Benefits: Understanding the psychological mechanisms behind gratitude can help individuals harness its benefits to foster resilience, reduce stress, and promote mental health.

3. Biblical Command and Spiritual Growth

Biblical teachings emphasize gratitude as a vital component of spiritual life and growth.

- Faith and Thanksgiving: Integrating gratitude into prayer and worship deepens one's relationship with God and enhances spiritual well-being.

- Contentment and Peace: Biblical wisdom encourages contentment through gratitude, fostering a sense of peace and trust in God's provision and plan.

Gratitude is a powerful and transformative practice that enriches our lives, strengthens our relationships, and enhances our well-being. By exploring gratitude through the lenses of ancient and modern philosophy, psychology, and biblical teachings, we can gain a deeper appreciation of its significance and integrate it more fully into our daily lives. As we cultivate a grateful heart, we open ourselves to greater joy, contentment, and spiritual growth, ultimately leading to a more fulfilling and harmonious existence.

Gratitude, a universal virtue, has been cherished across various philosophical traditions for centuries. Recognized for its profound impact on human well-being and social harmony, gratitude transcends cultural and temporal boundaries. This chapter explores the psychological benefits of practicing gratitude, supported by biblical wisdom, specifically focusing on the verse from 1 Thessalonians 5:18: "Give thanks in all circumstances; for this is God's will for you in Christ Jesus."

The Psychological Benefits of Practicing Gratitude

Gratitude, more than just a fleeting emotion, is a practice that can significantly enhance mental and physical health. Modern psychology has extensively studied the effects of gratitude, revealing its profound impact on various aspects of well-being.

1. Enhanced Mental Health

Gratitude has been linked to numerous positive mental health outcomes. Research in positive psychology highlights several ways in which gratitude improves mental health:

- Reduction in Depression and Anxiety: Studies have shown that gratitude practices can lead to significant reductions in symptoms of depression and anxiety. By focusing on positive aspects of life and expressing thankfulness, individuals can shift their attention away from negative thoughts and emotions.

- Increased Happiness and Life Satisfaction: Regularly practicing gratitude can boost overall happiness and satisfaction with life. This increase in positive affect is often sustained over time, contributing to long-term well-being.

2. Improved Physical Health

The benefits of gratitude extend beyond mental health, influencing physical well-being as well:

- Better Sleep: Grateful individuals tend to sleep better and for longer durations. The positive emotions associated with gratitude can create a more restful and relaxing pre-sleep environment, leading to improved sleep quality.

- Enhanced Immunity: Emerging research suggests that gratitude can strengthen the immune system. Grateful people exhibit healthier behaviors, such as regular exercise and balanced diets, which contribute to overall physical health.

- Reduced Stress and Inflammation: Chronic stress is a major contributor to various health problems. Practicing gratitude has been shown to reduce stress levels and, consequently, lower inflammation in the body.

3. Strengthened Relationships

Gratitude plays a crucial role in building and maintaining healthy relationships:

- Increased Empathy and Reduced Aggression: Grateful individuals are more likely to exhibit empathy and kindness towards others. This increased prosocial behavior can reduce aggression and conflict in relationships.

- Enhanced Social Bonds: Expressing gratitude to others strengthens social connections and fosters a sense of belonging. People who regularly show appreciation to their friends, family, and colleagues experience more positive interactions and stronger social ties.

4. Personal Growth and Resilience

Gratitude can also contribute to personal growth and resilience, helping individuals navigate life's challenges with greater ease:

- Increased Resilience: Grateful individuals tend to be more resilient in the face of adversity. By focusing on what they have rather than what they lack, they can maintain a positive outlook and find strength to overcome difficulties.

- Greater Sense of Purpose: Practicing gratitude can enhance one's sense of purpose and meaning in life. Recognizing and appreciating the good in life fosters a deeper connection to one's values and goals, leading to greater fulfillment.

Gratitude Practices

There are several effective ways to cultivate gratitude in daily life. These practices can help individuals harness the psychological benefits of gratitude:

1. Gratitude Journaling

Keeping a gratitude journal involves regularly writing down things for which one is thankful. This simple practice can have profound effects on well-being by shifting focus to positive aspects of life.

- Daily Reflection: Set aside time each day to reflect on and record three to five things you are grateful for. This consistent practice can help reinforce a positive mindset.

- Gratitude Letters: Writing letters of gratitude to significant individuals in your life can enhance both your own happiness and that of the recipient. Expressing appreciation strengthens relational bonds and promotes positive emotions.

2. Mindful Gratitude

Incorporating gratitude into mindfulness practices can deepen the experience of thankfulness and present-moment awareness:

- Gratitude Meditation: During meditation, focus on things you are grateful for. This practice can enhance emotional regulation and promote a sense of peace and contentment.

- Mindful Acknowledgment: Throughout the day, take moments to mindfully acknowledge and appreciate positive experiences and interactions. This can help you stay grounded in gratitude amidst daily activities.

3. Acts of Kindness

Engaging in acts of kindness is a powerful way to cultivate gratitude. Helping others not only benefits the recipients but also fosters a sense of thankfulness and satisfaction in the giver.

- Random Acts of Kindness: Perform small, spontaneous acts of kindness for others. These can range from offering a compliment to a stranger to helping a neighbor in need.

- Volunteer Work: Dedicating time to volunteer for a cause you care about can deepen your sense of gratitude and purpose.

Biblical Perspective on Gratitude

The Bible places a strong emphasis on the importance of gratitude, presenting it as a fundamental aspect of spiritual life and a reflection of one's relationship with God. The verse from 1 Thessalonians 5:18, "Give thanks in all circumstances; for this is God's will for you in Christ Jesus," underscores the significance of maintaining a thankful heart in every situation.

1. Gratitude as an Expression of Faith

Gratitude in the Bible is closely linked with faith and trust in God's plan:

- Trusting in God's Goodness: By giving thanks in all circumstances, believers express their trust in God's goodness and sovereignty. This attitude of gratitude reflects a deep faith that God is working for their ultimate good.

- Worship and Thanksgiving: Gratitude is an essential part of worship, acknowledging God's blessings and provision. Regularly expressing thankfulness strengthens one's relationship with God and fosters spiritual growth.

2. Gratitude and Contentment

The Bible teaches that gratitude fosters contentment and wards off feelings of envy and discontent:

- Philippians 4:6-7: "Do not be anxious about anything, but in every situation, by prayer and petition, with thanksgiving, present your requests to God. And the peace of God, which transcends all understanding, will guard your hearts and your minds in Christ Jesus." This passage highlights the role of gratitude in achieving inner peace and contentment.

- 1 Timothy 6:6-8: "But godliness with contentment is great gain. For we brought nothing into the world, and we can take nothing out of it. But if we have food and clothing, we will be content with that." Gratitude for basic necessities fosters a sense of contentment and reduces materialistic desires.

Integrating Psychological and Biblical Insights

Combining psychological research with biblical teachings provides a comprehensive understanding of gratitude and its transformative power.

1. Psychological Practices and Spiritual Growth

Psychological research offers practical strategies for cultivating gratitude, while biblical teachings provide a spiritual foundation for these practices:

- Gratitude Journaling and Prayer: Integrating gratitude journaling with prayer can deepen one's spiritual practice. Writing down things you are thankful for and presenting them to God in prayer reinforces both psychological and spiritual well-being.

- Acts of Kindness and Christian Service: Engaging in acts of kindness as a form of Christian service enhances gratitude while fulfilling the biblical call to love and serve others.

2. Mental and Emotional Benefits

Understanding the psychological benefits of gratitude can motivate individuals to incorporate it into their daily lives, supported by biblical encouragement:

- Resilience and Faith: Recognizing that gratitude fosters resilience can help believers maintain faith and trust in God's plan during difficult times.

- Contentment and Peace: Embracing gratitude as a path to contentment aligns with biblical teachings, promoting a sense of peace and fulfillment in God's provision.

Gratitude is a powerful and transformative practice that enriches our lives, strengthens our relationships, and enhances our well-being. By exploring gratitude through the lenses of psychology and biblical teachings, we can gain a deeper appreciation of its significance and integrate it more fully into our daily lives. As we cultivate a grateful heart, we open ourselves to greater joy, contentment, and spiritual growth, ultimately leading to a more fulfilling and harmonious existence.

CHAPTER 20

THE LEGACY OF THOUGHT

Thoughts shape not only the present but also leave a profound legacy for future generations. The impact of our thinking extends beyond personal and contemporary spheres, influencing societies, cultures, and intellectual traditions across time. This chapter explores the enduring impact of thought on future generations through the lens of various philosophical traditions, illustrating how ideas have shaped and continue to shape the world.

The Enduring Impact of Thought

Philosophy has long recognized the power of thought to influence the course of history and the development of civilizations. Philosophers from different traditions have emphasized the transformative potential of ideas, underscoring their ability to transcend temporal boundaries and leave a lasting legacy.

1. The Classical Philosophical Traditions

Classical philosophers, such as Plato and Aristotle, profoundly understood the enduring impact of thought. Their contributions to ethics, politics, metaphysics, and epistemology have shaped Western intellectual history for centuries.

- Plato: Plato's dialogues, particularly "The Republic," explore the nature of justice, the role of the philosopher-king, and the theory of forms. His ideas on idealism and the importance of philosophical inquiry have influenced countless thinkers and continue to resonate in contemporary philosophy.

- Aristotle: Aristotle's works on logic, metaphysics, ethics, and politics have been foundational to Western thought. His emphasis on empirical observation and the development of systematic knowledge laid the groundwork for scientific inquiry and rational discourse.

2. Eastern Philosophical Traditions

Eastern philosophical traditions, such as Confucianism and Buddhism, also highlight the enduring impact of thought on individual and societal well-being.

- Confucius: Confucian philosophy emphasizes the cultivation of virtue, ethical conduct, and social harmony. Confucius's teachings on filial piety, the role of the ruler, and the importance of education have deeply influenced Chinese culture and continue to guide moral and social practices in East Asia.

- Buddha: The teachings of the Buddha, particularly the concepts of mindfulness, compassion, and the Four Noble Truths, have had a profound impact on spiritual and philosophical traditions in Asia. Buddhism's emphasis on the transformation of the mind and the pursuit of enlightenment continues to inspire individuals and communities worldwide.

3. Enlightenment and Modern Thought

The Enlightenment era marked a significant shift in philosophical thought, emphasizing reason, individualism, and scientific inquiry. Thinkers such as Immanuel Kant and John Locke contributed to the development of modern philosophy, shaping contemporary understandings of knowledge, ethics, and governance.

- Kant: Immanuel Kant's "Critique of Pure Reason" and "Critique of Practical Reason" revolutionized philosophy by exploring the limits of human knowledge and the nature of moral autonomy. His ideas on the categorical imperative and the autonomy of reason continue to influence ethical and political theory.

- Locke: John Locke's "Two Treatises of Government" and "An Essay Concerning Human Understanding" laid the foundations for modern political philosophy and epistemology. His theories on natural rights, government by consent, and the separation of powers have been instrumental in shaping democratic institutions and liberal thought.

Thought and Cultural Transmission

The transmission of thought across generations is facilitated by various cultural institutions, including education, literature, and art. These mediums serve as vessels for the preservation and dissemination of ideas, ensuring their continuity and relevance.

1. Education

Education plays a crucial role in the transmission of thought, fostering intellectual growth and cultural continuity. Philosophers such as John Dewey have emphasized the importance of education in shaping democratic societies and nurturing critical thinking.

- Dewey: John Dewey's philosophy of education, as articulated in works like "Democracy and Education," advocates for experiential learning, critical inquiry, and the development of democratic dispositions. His ideas have influenced educational practices and policies worldwide, emphasizing the role of education in fostering a thoughtful and engaged citizenry.

2. Literature

Literature serves as a powerful medium for the transmission of thought, encapsulating cultural values, ethical dilemmas, and philosophical insights. The works of literary giants like Shakespeare, Tolstoy, and Achebe continue to resonate with readers, offering timeless reflections on the human condition.

- Shakespeare: William Shakespeare's plays and sonnets explore themes of love, power, betrayal, and identity, offering profound insights into human nature. His works have been adapted and interpreted across cultures, underscoring the universal relevance of his thought.

- Tolstoy: Leo Tolstoy's novels, such as "War and Peace" and "Anna Karenina," delve into the complexities of morality, social change, and personal transformation. His philosophical inquiries into nonviolence and spirituality continue to inspire readers and thinkers.

- Achebe: Chinua Achebe's "Things Fall Apart" addresses the impacts of colonialism and cultural change on African societies. His works highlight the importance of preserving cultural heritage and understanding the diverse legacies of thought across the globe.

3. Art

Artistic expression provides a visual and sensory representation of philosophical ideas, capturing the essence of cultural and intellectual movements. From the Renaissance to contemporary art, the visual arts have been instrumental in conveying complex thoughts and emotions.

- Renaissance Art: The Renaissance period witnessed a revival of classical thought, with artists like Leonardo da Vinci and Michelangelo blending artistic innovation with philosophical inquiry. Their works reflect the integration of beauty, proportion, and intellectual depth.

- Contemporary Art: Modern and contemporary artists continue to explore philosophical themes, challenging perceptions and provoking critical reflection. The works of artists like Marina Abramović and Ai Weiwei engage with issues of identity, freedom, and social justice, leaving a lasting impact on cultural discourse.

The Legacy of Thought in Action

The enduring impact of thought is not confined to intellectual pursuits; it extends to social and political action, influencing movements for justice, equality, and human rights. Visionary thinkers have inspired transformative change, demonstrating the power of ideas to shape the course of history.

1. Social and Political Movements

Philosophical thought has been a driving force behind social and political movements, advocating for justice, freedom, and human dignity.

- Gandhi: Mahatma Gandhi's philosophy of nonviolent resistance, rooted in principles of truth and non-harm, inspired movements for independence and civil rights. His legacy continues to influence advocates of social justice and peaceful protest.

- Martin Luther King Jr.: Martin Luther King Jr.'s advocacy for civil rights and his vision of the "Beloved Community" was deeply informed by philosophical and theological thought. His speeches and writings remain a powerful testament to the enduring impact of ideas on social change.

2. Environmental and Ethical Thought

Philosophical reflections on ethics and the environment have shaped contemporary discussions on sustainability and ecological responsibility.

- Rachel Carson: Rachel Carson's "Silent Spring" brought attention to the environmental impacts of chemical pesticides, sparking the modern environmental movement. Her work underscores the importance of ethical consideration in scientific and technological advancement.

- Peter Singer: Peter Singer's contributions to bioethics and animal rights have challenged conventional views on the moral status of non-human beings. His advocacy for utilitarian ethics and the reduction of suffering continues to influence ethical debates and policy decisions.

The legacy of thought is a testament to the enduring power of ideas to shape human experience and influence future generations. From classical philosophers to contemporary thinkers, the transmission of thought through education, literature, art, and social action ensures the continuity of intellectual and cultural heritage. By reflecting on the profound impact of thought, we can appreciate the responsibility we bear in cultivating and preserving ideas that promote wisdom, justice, and human flourishing.

The power of thought extends beyond the immediate present, influencing future generations and shaping the legacy we leave behind. In this chapter, we delve into the psychological aspects of how our thoughts influence legacy and generativity. By exploring theories of generativity and the impact of our mental processes on the legacy we create, we can better understand the profound responsibility and opportunity inherent in our thinking. This exploration is anchored by the biblical wisdom from Psalm 112:6, "The righteous will be remembered forever."

The Psychology of Legacy and Generativity

1. The Concept of Generativity

Generativity, as defined by Erik Erikson, is a concern for establishing and guiding the next generation. This stage, which typically occurs during middle adulthood, involves a focus on contributing to the welfare of others through parenting, teaching, mentoring, and community involvement. Generativity is a crucial aspect of psychological development, highlighting the importance of leaving a positive legacy.

- Erik Erikson's Theory: Erikson's psychosocial development theory places generativity versus stagnation as a critical conflict in middle adulthood. Generative individuals are those who invest in the growth and development of others, thereby ensuring the continuation of values, skills, and traditions.

- Influence on Future Generations: Generative actions, rooted in positive and constructive thoughts, have a lasting impact on future generations. These actions foster a sense of continuity and purpose, contributing to the overall well being of society.

2. Cognitive and Emotional Aspects of Legacy

The thoughts and emotions we cultivate play a significant role in shaping the legacy we leave behind. Positive thoughts and emotions enhance our ability to contribute meaningfully to the lives of others, while negative thoughts can hinder our generative efforts.

- Positive Thinking: Positive thoughts, characterized by optimism, hope, and resilience, enable individuals to overcome challenges and pursue long-term goals. These thoughts encourage actions that build a lasting and positive legacy.

- Emotional Intelligence: Emotional intelligence, the ability to recognize and manage our own emotions and the emotions of others, is critical in fostering generativity. High emotional intelligence facilitates empathy, effective communication, and conflict resolution, all of which are essential for creating a positive legacy.

3. The Role of Mindfulness and Intentionality

Mindfulness and intentionality are key components in shaping our legacy. By being mindful of our thoughts and actions and intentional in our efforts to contribute positively to the world, we can ensure that our legacy reflects our values and aspirations.

- Mindfulness: Mindfulness involves being present and fully engaged in the current moment. Practicing mindfulness helps individuals develop a deeper awareness of their thoughts and actions, allowing them to make conscious choices that align with their values and goals.

- Intentionality: Being intentional means setting clear, purposeful goals and working towards them with determination and focus. Intentional individuals are more likely to engage in generative activities that have a lasting impact on others.

The Impact of Thought on Legacy

1. Legacy Through Relationships

The relationships we build and nurture are a significant aspect of our legacy. Positive thoughts and emotions contribute to healthy, supportive relationships that can influence future generations.

- Family and Parenting: Positive parenting practices, grounded in thoughts of love, patience, and understanding, leave a lasting impact on children. These practices help children develop into responsible, caring adults who can, in turn, create their own positive legacies.

- Mentorship and Leadership: Mentors and leaders who approach their roles with thoughts of encouragement, inspiration, and guidance can significantly impact the lives of those they mentor. Their influence can extend far beyond the immediate relationship, shaping the future paths of many individuals.

2. Legacy Through Contributions to Society

Our thoughts drive our actions, which in turn shape our contributions to society. Whether through professional achievements, community service, or creative endeavors, the legacy we leave is a reflection of our thoughts and beliefs.

- Professional Achievements: Positive thoughts such as innovation, determination, and a desire to make a difference can lead to significant professional contributions. These achievements can leave a lasting mark on industries, organizations, and communities.

- Community Service: Thoughts of compassion, justice, and altruism motivate individuals to engage in community service. These actions can improve the quality of life for many people, creating a legacy of kindness and generosity.

- Creative Endeavors: Artistic and intellectual contributions, driven by thoughts of creativity and exploration, can inspire and educate future generations. The works of artists, writers, and thinkers often have enduring value, influencing cultural and intellectual landscapes for years to come.

Biblical Perspective on Legacy

The Bible provides profound insights into the importance of thoughts and legacy. Psalm 112:6 states, "The righteous will be remembered forever," highlighting the enduring impact of a virtuous life.

1. Righteousness and Legacy

Righteousness, characterized by moral integrity and ethical behavior, is foundational to creating a lasting legacy. The Bible emphasizes that the thoughts and actions of righteous individuals have an enduring impact, remembered and honored by future generations.

- Proverbs 13:22: "A good person leaves an inheritance for their children's children." This verse underscores the importance of thinking beyond the immediate present and considering the long-term impact of our actions on future generations.

- Matthew 5:16: "Let your light shine before others, that they may see your good deeds and glorify your Father in heaven." The thoughts that inspire good deeds not only create a positive legacy but also bring glory to God.

2. The Power of Positive Thoughts in Scripture

The Bible encourages believers to cultivate positive thoughts, which in turn lead to positive actions and a lasting legacy.

- Philippians 4:8: "Finally, brothers and sisters, whatever is true, whatever is noble, whatever is right, whatever is pure, whatever is lovely, whatever is admirable—

if anything is excellent or praiseworthy—think about such things." This verse highlights the importance of focusing on positive thoughts, which ultimately shape our actions and legacy.

- Colossians 3:2: "Set your minds on things above, not on earthly things." By focusing our thoughts on higher, spiritual values, we can create a legacy that transcends the material and temporal.

The legacy we leave is profoundly influenced by our thoughts. By cultivating positive thoughts, practicing mindfulness and intentionality, and engaging in generative actions, we can create a lasting and meaningful impact on future generations. The wisdom of the Bible, coupled with psychological insights, underscores the importance of thinking righteously and acting with purpose. As we reflect on our thoughts and their legacy, we are reminded of the enduring truth that "The righteous will be remembered forever" (Psalm 112:6).